Your guide to the

STRANGEST
TOURS IN BRITAIN

- and the best worldwide -

FRONT COVER PICTURES

top left - Sedlec Ossuary - page 92
top right - Witchery Tours - page 30
bottom left - Key Underwood Coon Dog Memorial Graveyard - page 52
bottom right - The Mystery Spot - page 43

STRANGEST
TOURS IN BRITAIN
- and the best worldwide -

TITLE NUMBER 2. FIRST EDITION.

WRITTEN & PUBLISHED BY
STRANGEST BOOKS

ACKNOWLEDGEMENTS

Thanks are given to those people who have kindly provided some of the photographs for inclusion
in this book. These photographs are reproduced with the permission of the relevant copyright holders.
Certain images appear from public domain.

This book is the result of extensive research and the entries contained herein are inserted at the sole
discretion of the publishers. This does not indicate a preference over establishments not included.
The publishers receive no payments or inducements for inclusion in this book.

foreword

Most of us can clearly remember a time when we saw or read about something that was so strange or unusual it made us gasp in wonder, or even sent a cold chill through our body.

   The Strangest series of Books has the very best compilations of all that is weird, amazing and bizarre in Britain (and the rest of the world) today, and will open up a wonderland of curiosities for you to discover - most of which you probably never knew existed.

   Each of the books in our series covers a chosen subject and will provide you with a thoroughly entertaining read. There are fascinating, mysterious, and very often unbelievable places and things to be seen. Some are so unusual that only a visit to actually see for yourself will suffice, or you can simply experience an unforgettable bedtime read, and then amaze your friends and colleagues with some of the startling facts.

   Sure to provide readers with as much pleasure as they did for the researchers, the Strangest series of Books can be purchased or ordered from all good book stores and high street retailers. Information on how to order direct can be found on page 96.

The world is a book and those who
do not travel read only one page.

- St.Augustine

about this book

Tours . . . . the very name conjures up images of a rock band or chart topping singer on their travels, playing to their faithful fan base in different parts of the world. But tours of visitor attractions, well, there are countless places in every country where visitors can view interesting attractions, and with modern technology and building techniques there are tours you can choose from on almost any subject springing up all the time.

As people can be mystified by the mysterious, amused by the absurd, or exhilarated by something exciting, this book, Strangest Tours in Britain *and the best worldwide*, is dedicated to providing readers with the most unusual and exciting tours there are. Read all about the chapel decorated with the bones of 40,000 skeletons, and the well where everyday items turn to stone. Or what about the gravest of graveyards, or the startling Mystery Spot. Then there is the house made of paper, the village made from bottles, and the castle made from coral.

Find out about freak shows, the Infinity Room, a man-made ocean, the penis restaurant, and the Winchester Mystery House where nothing is what it seems. From adventurous and thrilling tours, to sublime or ridiculous tours, they are all here in a book you will want to read more than once - Strangest Tours in Britain *and the best worldwide.*

alphabetical index of entries

Part One - BRITAIN

LEICESTERSHIRE
National Space Centre, Leicester - largest space attraction in the country - page 25

LONDON
Highgate Cemetery, N1 - tour of the tombs - page 27
London Duck Tours, SE1 - tour the capital in an amphibious vehicle - page 33
Thames Barrier Visitors Centre, SE18 - 4 x 3,700 ton water gates - page 38
Astral Travels, W1 - crop circle tours - page 17
Pet Cemetery, W2 - pets at peace - page 27

NORFOLK
Dinosaur Adventure Park, Norwich - t-rex and the lost world maze - page 19

NORTHAMPTONSHIRE
Rushton Triangular Lodge, Rushton - the significance of number 3 - page 32

NOTTINGHAMSHIRE
NCCL Galleries of Justice, Nottingham - 3 centuries of crime & punishment - page 36
The Tales of Robin Hood, Nottingham - robin and his band of merry men - page 40

SCOTLAND
Witchery Tours, Edinburgh - ghosts, gore and torture - page 30
Sharmanka Kinetic Theatre, Glasgow - ghoulish russian extravaganza - page 28
Loch Ness 2000, Inverness-shire - nessie in detail - page 16

SOMERSET & BRISTOL
Bizzare Bath Comedy Walk, Bath - hysterical walking tour - page 31

STAFFORDSHIRE
Ceramica, Stoke-on-Trent - magic carpet ride - page 26

SUSSEX
Brighton Sewers Tour, Brighton - you won't get flushed on this tour - page 18

TYNE & WEAR
National Glass Centre, Sunderland - 4,600 people on a glass roof - page 31

WARWICKSHIRE
Falstaffs Experience, Stratford-upon-Avon - plague cottage and more - page 22
Stratford Butterfly Farm, Stratford-upon-Avon - insects galore - page 38

YORKSHIRE
Mother Shipton's Cave
       & The Petrifying Well, Knaresborough - objects turn to stone - page 14
Wellington Lodge, Scarborough - llama trekking - page 25
In Search of Dracula Tour, Whitby - vampire vacation - page 36
Jorvik, York - float through the air in a time capsule - page 36

Part Two - USA

ALABAMA
Key Underwood Coon Dog Memorial Graveyard - coon dog cemetery - page 52

CALIFORNIA
The Mystery Spot - bizarre magic spot - page 43
The Winchester Mystery House - strangest house in the world - page 50
Vampire Tour of San Francisco - award winning vampire tour - page 61
Grandma Prisbrey's Bottle Village - complete village made out of bottles - page 63
Dearly Departed Tours - notorious locations tour - page 65
Crystal Cathedral - biggest glass building in the world - page 68
San Francisco Zoo Valentine's Day Sex Tours - animals on heat - page 69

COLORADO
Vic's Gold Panning - gold prospecting by the hour - page 71

FLORIDA
Miami Duck Tours - amphibious tour of the city - page 57
Coral Castle - amazing castle made out of 1,000's tons of coral - page 58
Gatorland - snappy show of prehistoric beasties - page 64
Zero Gravity Corporation - weightless trips to the upper atmosphere - page 66

HAWAII
Hawaii Volcano Hiking Tours - hottest tours in the world - page 46
Atlantis Adventures - passenger submarine tours - page 49
LOUISIANA
New Orleans Cemetery & Gris-Gris Walking Tour - voodoo cemetery tour - page 56

MASSACHUSETTS
The Paper House - house made out of newspapers - page 45

MICHIGAN
Hoegh Pet Casket Company - funeral arrangements for fido - page 69

NEW YORK
Sideshows by the Seashore - roll-up for the freak show - page 44
Elmira Bigfoot Search Tours -   tracking the sasquatch - page 72

OKLAHOMA
Violent Skies Tours - tornado, hurricane & water spout chasing - page 70

OREGON
The Oregon Vortex & House of Mystery - strange place of illusions - page 43

PENNSYLVANIA
Cabela's - the serengeti in a supermarket - page 67

SOUTH CAROLINA
Bulldog Tours Ghost & Graveyard Tour - themed graveyard tour - page 65

Part Three - REST OF WORLD

ITALY
South Tyrol Museum of Archaeology - otzi the iceman - page 81
Ancient Roman Sewers-Cloaca Maxima - world's oldest sewer - page 82

JAPAN
Tobu World Square - 140,000 mini people in the land of the rising sun - page 95
Ocean Dome Seagaia - man-made ocean - page 88

KOREA
Panmunjom & DMZ Tour - demilitarized border tour - page 84

NEW ZEALAND
Stuart Landsborough's Puzzling World - eccentric world of illusions - page 87

SOUTH AFRICA
Unrealdive - shark cage diving in shark alley - page 83

THAILAND
The Million Years Stone Park & Pattaya Crocodile Farm - 1,000's of crocs - page 77

Part One
- BRITAIN -

Mad Monk of Cowgate - page 30.

MOTHER SHIPTON'S CAVE & THE PETRIFYING WELL

Prophecy Lodge, High Bridge, Knaresborough, Yorkshire
Tel: 01423 864600

Mother Shipton is England's most famous Prophetess who lived some 500 years ago during the reigns of King Henry VIII and Queen Elizabeth I. The cave, her legendary birthplace, is near to the amazing geological phenomenon known as The Petrifying Well where magical cascading waters turn items into stone.

The cave itself is a collapsed flowstone deposit which was originally created over 12,000 years ago by the same waters that now flow over The Petrifying Well. Nobody knows for certain the circumstances that surround the birth of a child in 1488 in a cave beside the River Nidd, but it is said that a great crack of thunder and the smell of sulphur greeted the birth as the child came into the world. This child was to grow into a woman whose prophetic visions became feared throughout England, with many of them proving accurate today. A great many books have been written on the subject but none have explained the amazing powers of prophesy that Mother Shipton possessed. Her reputation spread way beyond Yorkshire and many believed she had mystical, even devilish powers.

Mother Shipton died at the beginning of Queen Elizabeth I's long reign and it is said that she even predicted her own death in 1561. She was buried in unconsecrated ground somewhere on the outskirts of York.

The Petrifying Well is England's oldest visitor attraction which first opened its gates in 1630. The waters form a spring behind The Petrifying Well and flow over the top at the rate of 3,200 litres per hour, and the spring has never been known to dry up. Over the years millions of people have come to see the miraculous powers of the Well and it is believed to be the only one of its kind in England. At the time Mother Shipton was born, Knaresborough people believed the Well to be magic as objects were known to be turned to stone in its falling waters. People were very superstitious in those days and believed that they too would be turned to stone if they ventured near it.

In the early 1600's samples of the water were examined by a medical physician whose report stated that waters from the Well were 'a miracle cure for any flux of the body'. It is only in the last 150 years or so that scientific analysis has revealed exactly what is behind the mysterious petrification process. The rock formation is one huge mineral deposit formed in much the same way as a stalactite would be. The waters come from a mile underground and travel along certain layers of rock from which they dissolve massive amounts of minerals. This high mineral content means that subsequently everything in its path is turned to stone.

Today, visitors to The Petrifying Well can see a host of everyday items that have been turned to stone including the shoe of Queen Mary who visited in 1923. Other items from TV soap stars, and even John Wayne's hat are on display in the museum here - set in stone.

Mother Shipton's Cave.

The Petrifying Well.

LOCH NESS 2000
**Loch Ness Centre,
Drumnadrochit,
Inverness-shire, Scotland
Tel: 01456 450573**

Whether you are a believer or a sceptic there is no getting away from the fact that the legend of the Loch Ness Monster still draws a huge global following and remains to this day one of Britain's greatest unsolved mysteries. Countless investigations, books, films and photographs, have yet to prove - or disprove - the monster's existence. The most common description of Nessie from eye-witness accounts is of a bulky creature with flippers and a long tapering neck and tail, with a general overall appearance of a Plesiosauras (an aquatic reptilian contemporary of the dinosaurs).

The loch itself is a tectonic lake, resulting from movements in the earths crust millions of years ago and is now the largest body of fresh water in Britain. In fact it contains more water than all the other lakes in England, Wales and Scotland put together.

Loch Ness 2000 is a hi-tech multi-media centre that charts the history of the monster and, perhaps more importantly, allows the visitor to gain an insight into important scientific findings whilst learning about Scotland and the ecology of a Scottish loch. Theories, possible explanations and legends can all be looked into here, together with the opportunity of participating in some research as well - on the Loch Ness Project's 'Deepscan' vessel.

CROP CIRCLE TOURS - ASTRAL TRAVELS UK TOURS

**72 New Bond Street,
London W1
Tel: 0700 0781 016 /
0870 9020 908**

Crop circles - bizarre geometric patterns within partially flattened fields of wheat and other such crops - have proved a puzzle that scientific experts and countless boffins have been unable to explain since they first appeared in Britain during the 1970's. Extraterrestrials, 'plasma vortices', and hoaxers are some of the many causes put forward for the phenomenon, but they remain an enigma to this day and no explanation has yet accounted for how grain stalks are bent, but not broken, and there are never traces of footprints leading to the crop circles.

Some of the stunning creations reported are said to cover an area of up to 250,000 sq ft, and since the early days they have evolved into amazing pictograms with some displaying intricate computer fractals and elements that could only be found in quantum physics processes.

Astral Travels include visits to some of the more striking crop circles in the west country on their 'Stones and Bones' tour, which also takes in other major attractions such as Stonehenge. Groups of people (any size) may also take advantage of private crop circle guided tours which actually takes you within the crop circles but please note that these are subject to season and availability.

Whoever or whatever is behind these astounding yet beautiful formations may never be known. The question is; are we truly alone?

Further reading: see 'The Barge Inn' featured in Strangest Pubs in Britain. Details on how to order see page 96.

BRIGHTON SEWERS TOUR

Brighton Pier, Brighton, Sussex
Tel: 0845 278 0845

Who would have thought a Victorian sewer system running underneath a seaside town could be marketed as a tourist attraction - yet Southern Water have pioneered this novel idea and it is probably the only one of its kind in the country.

Tours of the sewers, which take place from May to September, show many of the sewers still in use that were built by Victorian engineers when drainage in the town was first developed. The entrance to the sewers is through a pier arch below Brighton Palace Pier and, following a video showing, you are escorted into a world of distinctive smells and shadows. Pipes, tanks, shafts and tunnels are all part of a remarkably interesting tour which may be remembered next time you visit the bathroom. Rubber gloves and hard-hats are of course provided.

Although not common in the UK, sewer tours can be found in almost every other European country and in most instances are thriving visitor attractions. Read all about them on page 82.

THE DEEP

City Centre, Hull, Humberside
Tel: 01482 381000

First opened to the public in March 2002 The Deep is an underwater attraction like no other - a unique award winning aquarium that boasts over 3,500 fish and around 40 sharks. The educational and conservational charity behind The Deep is dedicated to increasing awareness of our oceans and visitors are transported on a fantastic journey of discovery to explore the wonders of the seas from tropical lagoons to the sub-zero waters of Antarctica.

The main tank contains 2.5 million litres of water and 87 tonnes of salt and a vast array of weird and wonderful marine life can be seen in the numerous aquatic exhibits. You can walk the ocean floor in what is said to be the world's deepest viewing tunnel whilst sharks glide effortlessly overhead, feel the ice cold walls of the Polar Gallery, visit the Twilight Zone exhibition, or ride in the scenic underwater lift surrounded by hundreds of exotic sea creatures such as Groupers and Rays. Pre-historic sea monsters can be seen on a dramatic fossil wall, and, from an educational viewpoint, you can discover what may be the future of our oceans and how they can be preserved for generations ahead.

Behind the scenes at The Deep a specialist team of marine biologists care for all the creatures in addition to their invaluable research into the marine environment.

DINOSAUR ADVENTURE PARK
**Western Park, Lenwade,
Norwich, Norfolk
Tel: 01603 876310**

Life size giants tower over you at Dinosaur Adventure Park. There are dinosaurs both huge and small lurking in the woods on the Trail here including Brachiosaurus, Stegosaurus, and the dreaded T-Rex. Visitors can help the ranger discover how many of these colossal beasts are roaming around in the woodland by using radios, lookout towers, and fieldstations.

   Another unique experience at Dinosaur Adventure Park is the 'Dinosculptor'. Watch him at work or view the amazing steel sculptures he has made including a life size T-Rex. There is much more to see and do here, particularly for youngsters, such as Raptor Racers, the Lost World Maze, and the Secret Animal Garden. Thrilling, educational and fun.

COMBE MARTIN WILDLIFE & DINOSAUR PARK
**Combe Martin, Ilfracombe,
Devon. Tel: 01271 882486**

Visit the land that time forgot - a sub tropical paradise featuring hundreds of animals and birds plus animatronic dinosaurs. Some are so real in appearance they seem alive! This is also the UK's only wolf research and education centre.

CREALY GREAT ADVENTURE PARK
**Sidmouth Road,
Clyst St.Mary, Exeter, Devon
Tel: 01395 233200**

Opened in 1985, Crealy Great Adventure Park has become a favourite year round attraction that is great whatever the weather - as 75,000 sq ft is under cover. There are numerous themed areas and attractions to explore, far too many to mention here, but Dina the baby Dinosaur and the Funsaurus Show gets the gold star.

The remarkable Eden Project.

EDEN PROJECT
Bodelva, St.Austell, Cornwall
Tel: 01726 811901

Opened to the public in 2001, the Eden Project was established as a landmark millenium project with a mission to promote the understanding and responsible management of the vital relationship between plants, people and resources, leading to a sustainable future for all. It is an epic and spectacular setting for one of the great marvels of modern Britain, being unique in design, planning and mission. This living theatre of plants and visitors is based in a 50 metre deep crater and houses 3 of the world's climate zones which in turn nurture thousands of the world's most important plants.

The 3 zones, or 'Biomes' as they are called, are the Humid Tropics (Rainforests and Tropical Islands), the Warm Temperate regions (the Mediterranean, South Africa and California) and the Outdoor Biome which is a temperate zone thriving on the climatic advantages of Cornwall and displaying a glorious range of plants from India, Russia, the Atlantic rainforests, and other regions. The first 2 Biomes are housed in 2 giant conservatories.

The 'Core' is perhaps the greatest moment in the project's history. Since being unveiled this superb modern building, constructed at a cost of £15 million, is the biggest and most instructive educational centre of its kind in the UK. The design is based on the fundamental rule of how plants grow. It has a central trunk with a canopy roof that shades the ground yet attracts the sun. The Core is awe-inspiring and fills the individual with a sense of perspective and harmony with nature.

The Eden Trust - which is the registered charity that owns the project - uses money raised to further the charitable aims of the Trust. If the future is not green then we simply don't have a future, so finding and promoting ways we can work within nature and caring more for how we treat our planet will always be priorities.

Cornwall is an extreme southwest area of England on a peninsula that is bounded by the English Channel and the Atlantic Ocean. Famous for its tin and copper mines Cornwall is almost an island, being surrounded by sea on most sides with the River Tamar which runs along much of the county line almost severing it from Devon.

The influence of the Gulf Stream, particularly in winter, means Cornwall's climate is milder than in any other part of Britain and spring begins early here with many flowers appearing at the beginning of the year. Autumn also lingers much longer than in other parts of the UK and the county generally gets over 1,500 hours of sunshine annually. Subtropical vegetation is evident along the southern coast. The mild climate of Cornwall permits the lush valleys to be most productive for dairy and vegetable farming, whilst sheep and cattle thrive here.

THE FALSTAFFS EXPERIENCE

**Sheep Street,
Stratford-upon-Avon,
Warwickshire
Tel: 0870 350 2770**

The Falstaffs Experience is believed to be one of the most haunted properties in Britain and they hold lantern lit Ghost Tours several evenings a week, in addition to 'Midnight Vigils' for the more fearless visitors. It is also regularly visited by teams of mediums, psychics and paranormal investigators. As a visitor attraction it is spooky, yet exciting and unusual, offering an educational and fun journey through time.

Situated in the 16th century Shrieves House Barn in the centre of Stratford upon Avon, The Falstaffs Experience will take you on a journey that tells of some remarkable tales of the history of Stratford and England. It is certainly a heady atmosphere that is felt by many who pass through its labyrinth of theatrical settings. The huge gates of The Shrieves House open to reveal many of its secrets, and a short walk along a cobbled courtyard will bring you up to this famous building. It has survived 2 great fires, the Plague and the Civil War. The building holds many mysteries and has secret chambers, priestholes, and much history.

The Tenement is a reconstruction of Emm's Court which was Stratford's most notorious slum. It lay directly opposite The Shrieves House and is a place of fear and superstition where danger is said to lurk in every shadow.

The Haunted Chamber is said to be thronged with the souls of luckless pilgrims from the days of the Reformation and they are often seen by visitors here.

The Plague Cottage has a harrowing history yet is a fascinating insight into the turbulent period of history it relates to. It is a realistic re-creation of a 16th century dwelling that recounts the effects of the Bubonic Plague.

The Witches Glade was where the dark arts were secretly conducted within the glades of the forest - away from the eyes of the dreaded Witchfinder General and his band of deadly regulators.

Stratford was in the thick of the battle during these times and The Civil War tells you about the atrocities of nearby Edgehill where the spirits of the dead are still said to clash on the haunted battlefield.

The Falstaffs Tavern is a re-creation of the very tavern that once stood on this site. The Civil War that raged across the country was discussed here, and the tense atmosphere and chinking of tankards is very much alive.

The Strange but Untrue section of your tour is filled with bizarre facts and antiquities skipping between truth and fiction. The more impossible it seems, the more realistic chance it is true. Superstition explores the bizarre rituals and beliefs through the ages, sometimes hilarious, sometimes creepy.

Finally, for all those who hanker for the real good old days, The Old Penny Arcade is a collection of nostalgic treats that will please all age groups. The antique machines include original pinball machines and even Madame Zandra's crystal ball. All in all a most interesting tour.

THE GNOME RESERVE
West Putford,
near Bradworthy, Devon
Tel: 01409 241435

Children of all ages and anyone young at heart cannot fail to be enchanted by this wonderland of delightful gnomes and pixies set in the splendour of a 4 acre reserve that comprises woodland, 100ft pond, meadows and up to 300 species of herbs, wild flowers and ferns. Over 1,000 of the little chaps (and lasses) reside here in this magical kingdom and can be seen in a variety of settings. There is so much to discover at The Gnome Reserve such as tiny pixies being individually modelled, fired in the kiln and hand painted. Or visit

the collection of early garden gnomes in the museum. Gnome hats are loaned to visitors free of charge together with fishing rods, and the whole experience is truly memorable. Be sure to take your camera when you visit The Gnome Reserve.

Plenty of space at the National Space Centre.

Llama trekking in Scarborough.

- star treks -

NATIONAL SPACE CENTRE
Exploration Drive, Leicester, Leicestershire
Tel: 0870 60 77223

This is the largest attraction in the country dedicated to astronomy and space science which offers an awe-inspiring journey to the stars that probably no living person on earth today will make in reality. Space rockets, capsules, satellites, hands-on activities and technology are all here to explore, and if you often wonder what the experience of being an astronaut entails then this is the place to find out. Test your reaction times, stress levels, and find out how you eat, sleep and go to the toilet whilst in space.

The Challenger Learning Centre - the only one of its kind outside of North America - allows you the opportunity to take on the role of an astronaut on a spacecraft or a scientist at mission control, whilst the Solar System can be viewed in superb technicolour and real Moon Rock and Martian Meteorites can be seen along with giant models of the planets. Jump on the planetary scales and you can find out how much you'd weigh on the Moon or Jupiter.

Space Now is an exhibition bursting with astral information bringing you all the latest news. Launches can be seen live on the big screen, there is a mission departures board, and workshops, debates and demonstrations are taking place all the time. The latest theories on how the universe began and how it might end are also addressed together with the burning question that

may never be answered; are we alone?

The Rocket Tower houses the Space Centre's largest rockets in addition to a Satellite Zoo containing numerous artefacts from around the world, and the different themed galleries provide an abundance of information and space related technology. Special events are held throughout the year at the National Space Centre such as 'Meet an Astronaut' day and are suitable for all the family.

WELLINGTON LODGE LLAMA TREKKING
Staintondale, Scarborough, Yorkshire
Tel: 01723 871234

Alert, quiet, inquisitive, mischievous - llamas may be one or all of these but there is no doubting that they are very individual characters. A private family business, Wellington Lodge offers unique llama treks over a variety of terrains that include coastal paths, valleys and moors. Whilst you enjoy the scenery and history your sure footed llama carries the food, drink and extra clothing. They operate throughout the year and offer a great choice of themed journeys such as the Smuggler's Trek, Dinosaur Trek, (unearthing genuine fossils), Roam with a Ranger Trek, and even a Wine or Champagne Trek that includes a 3 course meal.

- dish of the day -

GOONHILLY EARTH STATION
Goonhilly Downs, Helston, Cornwall. Tel: 0800 679593

With over 60 huge dishes making a striking impact on the Lizard Peninsula landscape, Goonhilly is both the oldest and largest Satellite Station on the planet and provides a unique opportunity to explore the world of international communications. Visitors are taken on a voyage of exploration and will discover why this enormous site exists, and why it is so vitally important. State of the art technology and interactive media will enable you to enjoy experiences unique to Goonhilly. Operate an antenna dish, see yourself in outer space, or view your own animated 3D virtual head!

Goonhilly is able to transmit to all corners of the globe through underground fibre optic cables and via space. It also simultaneously handles millions of international phone calls, television broadcasts and emails. The guided bus tour is superb and the Multimedia visitors centre provides plenty to see and do for almost any age group.

CERAMICA
Market Place, Burslem, Stoke-on-Trent, Staffordshire Tel: 01782 832001

Ceramica can be found in the heart of the English Potteries and has a plethora of fascinating displays, exhibitions, and hands-on experiences making it a brilliant learning centre for children, and a real eye-opener for adults. In Bizarreland you will learn how clay is transformed into china, and a Magic Carpet enables you to take a ride over the 'Mother Town' of Burslem. You can also listen to a studio potter's life and actually have a go at throwing your own pot on a potter's wheel.

The Pavillions is an exploration into the past, present and future of the ceramic industry with interactive displays. Wade, Royal Doulton, Sadlers, Royal Stafford and much more; find out about them all including testing and how they are made. You can even feel the heat of a bottle oven or have a go at designing your own ceramic pieces.

- rest in peace -

HIGHGATE CEMETERY
Swain's Lane, Highgate,
London N6
Tel: 0208 340 1834

In the early 19th century Parliament authorised the creation of 7 private cemeteries within inner London as burial conditions there had deteriorated drastically. Highgate West Cemetery was thus opened in 1839 and extended to incorporate the East Cemetery in 1854. Although becoming dilapidated over the years it is now owned and operated by a charity (the Friends of Highgate Cemetery) who have subsequently oversee a major conservation programme. Listed by English Heritage as of "outstanding historical and architectural interest" this Grade II stylistic woodland park enables numerous popular and rare wildlife species to flourish in an undisturbed setting. Over 50 species of bird and 18 species of butterfly co-exist here and copious amounts of planting within a set programme has seen well in excess of 100 different species of trees, flowers and shrubs thrive.

Hundreds of famous people are buried at Highgate including previous Lord Mayors of London, Fellows of the Royal Society, and many notables such as Karl Marx and Sir Ralph Richardson. It is believed that Highgate has the best collection of Victorian funerary architecture in the country; distinctive examples being the Lebanon Circle Vaults, Egyptian Avenue, and the Terrace Catacombs.

Hugely interesting tours are available but strictly by pre-booking only as Highgate is still a working cemetery.

PET CEMETERY
Victoria Gate, Hyde Park,
London W2
Tel: 0207 298 2117

Probably the most famous pet cemetery in the country this was built by the Duke of Cambridge in 1880 and is the final resting place of more than 300 animals including many royal pets. Many of the graves have moving epitaphs which clearly illustrates the love felt for these animals by their predominantly upper-class owners, and the great sense of loss that must have ensued following their deaths. Although now closed since becoming full, it was originally run by a Mr Windbridge who was the lodgekeeper at the time and the person who buried almost all the animals here. The majority were sewn up in canvas bags but a few were laid to rest in coffins. The cemetery may be visited when 'open house' weekend is held during September.

There are now many pet cemeteries in Britain including Rossendale in Lancashire where there are over 1,500 graves. Permission was previously granted by the local council to allow owners to be buried with their pets here, or have their ashes scattered on their pet's graves. Some pet cemeteries will have a Chapel of Rest whilst there are often facilities to hold a non-denominational Christian or non religious ceremony. Most churchyards do not permit animal burials and it is illegal in a human cemetery as animals are classified as controlled waste. Burial in your own garden is still the most common practice.

RUSHTON TRIANGULAR LODGE

Desborough Road, Rushton, Northamptonshire
Tel: 01536 710761

Rushton Triangular Lodge is one of very few triangular buildings in England and has a fascinating history that is quite unique, yet somewhat mysterious. The folly was designed and built by Sir Thomas Tresham (who was the father of one of the Gunpowder Plotters) between 1593 and 1597. Tresham was a Catholic who spent some 15 years in prison because of his beliefs, and he was also a mystic numerologist. On his release from prison in 1593 he designed Rushton

Triangular Lodge as a protestation of his faith. His belief in the Holy Trinity can be seen expressed throughout the building; in fact the whole design is based on the number 3.

The ground plan of the Lodge is a perfect equilateral triangle with each side 33ft long - said to be the age of Christ at his death. The building has 3 floors (each with 3 windows), 3 steep gables and gargoyles on each side, and a 3-sided obelisk at the apex. Even the main chimney is 3-sided. There are trefoil windows, and the Latin text inscriptions which run around each facade of the building each have 33 letters. The principal room on each of the floors is a hexagon, which leaves the 3 corner spaces triangular.

The Lodge is a prime example of Elizabethan popularity with allegory, but also a testament to the faith of Tresham. Among the emblems here is the symbolic, 7-branched candelabrum on the gables representing the 7 eyes of God. There is also a Pelican emblem which is a symbol of Christ and the Eucharist. Among the dates carved on the Lodge are 1580 (thought to be the date of Tresham's conversion), and 5555 (thought to have originally been 3333).

Tresham died in 1605 and this was the only building he designed. On the front entrance is the inscription 'Tres Testimonium Dant', meaning 'there are 3 that give witness'. This is a biblical quotation from the Gospel of St.John that refers to the Holy Trinity, but is also a twist on Tresham's name as his wife referred to him as 'Good Tres' in her letters. Although there are other larger triangular structures in Europe, such as the gigantic Chateau de Chantilly in France, few have the mystery of Rushton Triangular Lodge.

- by road and river -

LONDON DUCK TOURS
55 York Road, London SE1
Tel: 0207 928 3132

The most unique way to see London and its magnificent sights is on an amphibious vehicle known as a 'Duck' - or 'DUKW' as they were originally known when used in the D-Day landings. More than 21,000 were built to take the troops ashore, but today's vehicles are very different to their wartime predecessors.

Departing from County Hall, your 'Duck' tour (which lasts over an hour), with informative commentary, will take you past famous London landmarks before splashing into the Thames for the river part of the tour.

Baby hedgehogs need love and attention too and (below) The Amazing Hedge Puzzle (also known as The Jubilee Maze).

- hedges to hedgehogs -

THE AMAZING HEDGE PUZZLE

**Symonds Yat West,
Ross-on-Wye, Herefordshire
Tel: 01600 890360**

Created by avid maze enthusiasts Lindsay and Edward Heyes to commemorate the Queen's Silver Jubilee in 1977, The Amazing Hedge Puzzle (also known as The Jubilee Maze) is Herefordshire's most popular private tourist attraction. The shortest route to the centre is only 200yds but there are also another 11 routes. There are 13 dead-ends to negotiate and it is said that the paths wear down by 2 inches a year. With only a single escape-route from the centre it is little wonder. The hedges themselves are over 6ft high with the whole idea being not to confuse you but to have fun - shouting at each other 'over here' as in days of old when mazes were so popular. The route from the centre of the maze leads to the Museum of Mazes, an interactive area offering many puzzles and a chance to explore mazes from all over the world. Of the exhibitions, Mazes and Mysteries is about the history of mazes, whilst Mazes and Micros explores the future of mazes in relation to technology.

ESCOT FANTASY GARDENS, MAZE & WOODLAND

**Escot, Fairmile,
Ottery St.Mary, Devon
Tel: 01404 822188**

Originally set out as 220 acres of 'Capability Brown' parkland and gardens, visitors will find Escot an unbelievable place with crafts, birds of prey, wetlands, waterfowl, wild boar, tropical fish and a whole lot more. The 'Jurassic Park', upside-down trees, and of course the remarkable 4,000 Beech Tree Hedge Maze with 5 hedge-leaping bridges, a stunning lookout tower, and 4 hidden switch-gates to increase difficulty, all make a visit to Escot essential for the whole family.

HEDGEHOG HOSPITAL & BRITISH WILDLIFE CENTRE

**Prickly Ball Farm, Denbury Road, Newton Abbot, Devon
Tel: 01626 362319**

For a day out with a complete difference come and see the hedgehogs at Prickly Ball Farm. The busy 'hands-on' hospital helps hundreds of sick and injured hedgehogs every year who are brought in by the RSPCA or kind members of the public. You can see, touch and learn all about these prickly characters and in mid-season see the baby hogs feeding. Plenty of work is put into looking after these baby hogs, particularly those born late in the season, for if they do not weigh at least a pound in weight by October the majority will not survive hibernation unless taken indoors to be fed and cared for. You can see a village made for hedgehogs to use before their final release back into the wild, walk a truly delightful wildflower meadow, or try the Night Watch Hedgehog Safari (adults only) for an evening of prickly encounters with the animals.

- vampires, villains & vikings -

IN SEARCH OF DRACULA TOUR
Whitby, Yorkshire
Tel: 01947 821734

Known throughout the world and surpassing all other myths and legends in terms of fame, horror and notoriety is Dracula, a blood-sucking vampire, the mere mention of whose name still strikes fear into the hearts of countless people in many countries with historical links to the legend.

On the 'In Search of Dracula Tour' you will discover who Bram Stoker was, why he came to Whitby, and how Whitby came to be in the novel 'Dracula'. You will walk and talk where Dracula once stalked and see the point where he came ashore after killing the whole crew of the ship he arrived on. Tours are held most weekends and frequent weekday evenings departing from Whalebone Arch on the West Cliff. Private parties can be catered for with advance bookings. Call it a holiday experience if you will but be prepared for an experience you may never forget.

NCCL GALLERIES OF JUSTICE
High Pavement, The Lace Market, Nottingham, Nottinghamshire
Tel: 0115 952 0555

Situated on an historic site which was in use as courts and prisons from the 1780's to the 1980's is the NCCL (National Centre for Citizenship & The Law) Galleries of Justice, a unique award winning attraction that provides an atmospheric tour through 3 centuries of crime and punishment. A court has been on the site since at least 1375 and a prison since 1449. It is said that the dark corridors you travel through are haunted by the very poor souls who once occupied these buildings. Witness a real trial in the original Victorian Courtroom and put your friends or family in the dock to be sentenced, or view the original prison cells, medieval caves, laundry, or prison exercise yard. Prisoners and gaolers act as your guides through the tour where you will also find interactive exhibitions.

The 1833 wing at the NCCL Galleries of Justice is now the new home of a great exhibition which was previously kept hidden away. The collection of previously unseen artefacts from prisons across the country includes items related to prison labour, escapes and riots, execution and much more, providing a realistic insight into the sometimes brutal nature of life in prison for inmates (and prison staff) over the last 3 centuries.

JORVIK
Coppergate, York, Yorkshire
Tel: 01904 543403

Journey back over 1,000 years to see and hear the noises of the Jorvik Viking City from the marketplace to the blacksmith's furnace, and the houses and workshops to the streets and alleys. State-of-the-art time capsules float you through the sprawling settlements whilst the smoke from countless home fires drifts over the rooftops. This fantastic multi-million pound attraction has thousands of genuine Viking artefacts to view and is the most realistic experience you will have of Viking life as opposed to actually having lived at that time.

*Journey through 3 centuries
of crime and punishment   at
NCCL Galleries of Justice.*

- water wings -

THAMES BARRIER VISITORS CENTRE
Unity Way, Woolwich, London SE18
Tel: 0208 305 4188

London has suffered several major floods in its history including a major drama way back in 1236 where it is said that people could actually row across Westminster Hall. On another occasion (7th December 1663) Samuel Pepys wrote in his diary "There was last night the greatest tide that was ever remembered in England to have been in this river; all Whitehall having been drowned". As such there has long been a great need for protection from flood damage caused by the Thames and in 1974 work began on a project that was to take 10 years to complete, the end result being the massive Thames Barrier which is an engineering marvel.

The barrier is a series of 10 separate and movable gates which are positioned across the Thames, each one supported by concrete piers. When closed the barrier seals off part of the upper Thames from the sea and when not in use the rising gates are

housed out of sight in recessed concrete cills in the riverbed thus allowing river traffic to pass. At over 1,700ft in width with each of the 4 enormous main openings measuring 200ft the barrier is truly a sight to behold. Each main gate is a hollow steel plated structure that weights approximately 3,700 tonnes and they are capable of taking a load of over 9,000 tonnes individually.

Now ranked as a major London tourist attraction the Thames Barrier is best viewed from one of the many frequent boat trips that depart from Greenwich and Westminster Pier. The Visitors Centre has a superb exhibition chronicling not only the history of the Thames but also the construction of the barrier from concept to completion.

STRATFORD BUTTERFLY FARM
Swan's Nest Lane, Stratford-upon-Avon, Warwickshire
Tel: 01789 299288

Just a five minute stroll from the town centre is this unique attraction which is quite spectacular; hundreds of the world's most beautiful and colourful butterflies flying around in a tropical environment. In the Caterpillar Room you can see their short but amazing life cycles.

Regardless of the weather you can amble through the lush landscape of an exotic rainforest with waterfalls and fish filled pools, marvel at the industrious leaf-cutting ants and stick insects in Insect City, or brave the sights of the dangerous web spinners in Arachnoland - home of the world's largest spider, a scorpion colony, and much more.

- **38** -

BUCKFAST ABBEY
Buckfastleigh, Devon
Tel: 01364 645550

The community of Benedictine Monks who lead a life of work, prayer and study at Buckfast Abbey, always extend a kindly welcome to visitors. The sprawling complex that is Buckfast includes the church, monastery, education centre, restaurants and shops, in addition to lavender, sensory and physic gardens. There is even a post office here. The monastic produce shop is unique as it sells a huge variety of products made by monasteries and convents from all over the world. Preserves, soaps, fudge, candles, biscuits, fabrics . . . you name it and there is a good chance it is on sale here. Most famous of all the products at the shop is the Buckfast Tonic Wine. Originally this was a patented medicine brought over by French Monks when they re-established Buckfast Abbey in the late 19th century. Although the recipe has been developed over the years its production almost came to a full stop during the 1920's when it was deemed that a licence was needed to manufacture such a wine. Although the licence was refused by local magistrates an agreement was reached with a local wine merchant to bottle the Tonic Wine at his warehouses.

Founded almost 1,000 years ago, Buckfast Abbey stood for 500 years before it was closed by Henry VIII. The existing community of monks came back to Buckfast in 1882 and subsequently rebuilt the Abbey upon its medieval foundations. The church is rather more recent and was completed in 1938.

MONKEY WORLD
Longthorns, Wareham,
Dorset. Tel: 01929 462537

Monkey World houses the largest group of chimpanzees outside of Africa and although a tour here is not 'strange' in the context of this book, their behaviour certainly is. This is a sheer delight for people of all ages (children in particular) who can marvel at the relentless antics of these adorable creatures.

Set up in 1987 by Jim and Alison Cronin, the centre rescues and provides a refuge for abused monkeys - chimps in particular - who are then rehabilitated into social groups with plenty of care and attention. The monkeys are rescued from numerous countries, in many instances having suffered serious injuries or mistreatment, and are gently helped to regain their confidence and socialize again. The on-site hospital and operating theatre has specialist staff who are experts in primate health and rehabilitation.

Featured on numerous television programmes, Monkey World is home to about 15 different species of primates including chimpanzees, gibbons, marmosets, capuchins and orang-utans. The spacious enclosures and natural woodland settings encourages our closest living relatives to revert back to their natural behaviour in a secure environment. At the park, which covers 65 acres in Dorset, visitors will find an education centre, cafe and gift shop, pets enclosure, and of course an abundance of monkeys.

THE TALES OF ROBIN HOOD

**30-38 Maid Marian Way,
Nottingham, Nottinghamshire
Tel: 0115 948 3284**

Childhood memories come flooding back as we write about the man who was feared by the bad and loved by the good (as the television song lyrics went) - yes, its Robin Hood of course, the world's most famous outlaw who robbed the rich to give to the poor.

Step back in time at this super medieval adventure and experience the smells and sounds in a world of mystery and merriment as you ride in a unique adventure car. Legend and adventure abound here and the numerous activities will capture your imagination. The inspiration of story tellers for over 700 years, Robin Hood will forever be associated with Sherwood Forest. Older enthusiasts can enjoy a night of feasting and entertainment with Robin, his Maid Marian, and his Merry Men at Medieval Banquets held in the Grand Hall.

Part Two
- USA -

*This way for the haunted
Victorian manor house - page 60.*

*The enigma of The Mystery Spot
and (below) the House of
Mystery, part of the startling
Oregon Vortex.*

THE MYSTERY SPOT
**465 Mystery Spot Road,
Santa Cruz, California**

Millions of people from all over the world have by now visited The Mystery Spot - an area 150ft in diameter within the redwood forests - since it was first opened to the public in 1940. Theories abound as to the causes of this phenomenon and include 'biocosmic radiation', carbon dioxide seeping out of the earth, and even aliens that have buried 'guidance systems' here! Whatever the cause is it remains very much the same enigma since when it was first discovered in 1939.

Within The Mystery Spot you will be astounded as the laws of gravity and physics are seemingly non-existant. Perspective, height and velocity are also affected in a wild experience that science is at a loss to explain. Visitors apparently lean towards the southwest when entering the radius of The Mystery Spot and progressively lean more and more as they approach the centre of the spot. Another bizarre happening occurs when a level is set across 2 cement blocks that are identical in height. A person stands to one end of the level which is within the spot whilst the second person stands at the other end which is just outside the spot. Bizarrely, one of the people suddenly appears much taller.

THE OREGON VORTEX & HOUSE OF MYSTERY
4303 Sardine Creek L Fork Road, Gold Hill, Oregon

The strange world of The Oregon Vortex is a similar experience to the Mystery Spot and will challenge all your beliefs and theories regarding perception. Said to be a spherical field of force, half above and half below ground, much scientific research and analysis has been conducted into this phenomenon. The results, which comprises 30 or 40 pictures together with illustrations and scientific data, is available to all visitors. A vortex is essentially a powerful whirlpool and can be related to the basic structure of the universe, from a galaxy to the vortex of an atom.

Nowhere within The Oregon Vortex do you appear to be standing erect and whether magnetic influences are present here has yet to be proven but the effects remain quite startling.

The House of Mystery was originally an assay office built by the Old Grey Eagle Mining Company in 1904, but the history of the surrounding area known as The Oregon Vortex can be traced back to the Native Americans who called the area the 'Forbidden Ground' and refused to enter there. John Litster, a geologist, mining engineer and physicist, developed the area during the 1920's and opened it to the public in 1930. He conducted thousands of experiments within the area of The Oregon Vortex and House of Mystery itself until his death in 1959. It remains a mystery to this day.

COSMOS
near Keystone, South Dakota

Yet more mind-boggling disproportionate height irregularities similar to The Mystery Spot and The Oregon Vortex. This is rumoured to be the result of the workings of gravity as it is located on the side of a steep mountain but is still an experience that defies belief.

SIDESHOWS BY THE SEASHORE
1208 Surf Avenue, Brooklyn, New York

Located at the corner of Surf Avenue & West 12th Street in the centre of Coney Island Amusement Park is the long running exhibition of freaks, wonders and human curiosities called Sideshows By The Seashore (also previously known as 'Coney Island Freak Show'). The building was originally Child's Restaurant, which employed singing waiters, and during the 1950's and 1960's it was home to Dave Rosen's Wonderland Circus Sideshow featuring legendary acts such as Sealo the Seal Boy and Jack Dracula. The Sideshow may feature many startling, bizarre, or grotesque abnormalities of the human species, so be prepared. Recent performers such as Insectavora, Scott Baker (the Twisted Shockmeister), Bambi the Mermaid, Ula (the Painproof Rubber Girl), and The Human Blockhead would have been guaranteed to make you forget a toothache - or give you one!

Most people would remember P.T.Barnum as the man who was responsible for elevating side show circus freaks into an art, but it was Samuel W.Gumpertz who brought the freak show to the seashore. He somehow managed to convince 300 midgets from circuses and fairs around the world to join him in creating a midget city called 'Lilliputia' for the opening season of Dreamland at Coney Island in 1904. The success he enjoyed with 'Lilliputia' convinced him to make Coney Island his

permanent base and he set out to explore the world and return with the most grotesque specimens of human curiosities he could find. These included a tribe of over 200 poison-dart blowing Bantocs, and women from Burma who stretched their necks by over a foot in length. The public lapped it up and by 1908 he was made the general manager of Dreamland.

The Dreamland Circus Sideshow was set up in a 40ft x 80ft tent along Surf Avenue and Gumpertz convinced freaks and curiosities the world over to appear for him. Fat, thin, limbless or 3-legged, it mattered not to Gumpertz - the public loved it. Over the years the grotesqueness increased, as did the profits. Tens of thousands of spectators took the tour each summer day during the 1920's. Probably the most popular of all the freaks who entertained these vast crowds was Zip, the dark skinned American Negro, who had a tiny head and was said to be a creature from Africa. When Zip died in 1926, after a long life, his pallbearers included the 'Human Skeleton' and the 'Tattooed Lady'.

Shows over the years included a double-bodied man, 'Electricia' the electric lady, numerous dwarfs, plus the obligatory fat and bearded ladies. Of the many other attractions that amazed and astounded visitors were the 'Spider Boy', a 4-legged girl, and the 'Human Fountain' who gushed streams of water from his fingers and toes.

Gumpertz left Coney Island in 1929 to run the Barnum and Bailey Circus but the Sideshow carried on, despite dwindling crowds. It still exists to this day and is proof that nothing arouses human curiosity like a human curiosity.

THE PAPER HOUSE
52 Pigeon Hill Street,
Rockport, Massachusetts

In 1922 Elis F.Stenman started to build a summer house. Commencing with a wooden frame he then started to insulate the house with newspaper, but then had a thought; what if he built the whole house out of newspapers? Being a curious amateur inventor who liked to experiment with things, he then began a project that would take up 20 years of his life - building a paper house.

Newspapers cost little in those days and he made his own glue, which was basically flour and water with added sticky substances such as apple peel. After making the internal walls and roof, approximately an inch thick and made

out of layers and layers of newspaper with glue and varnish on the outside, he lived in the house whilst setting about making the furniture. Everything inside is made up of tight, rolled newspaper 'logs' which are stained and hardened. Chairs, table, display cabinets, even a piano (although this only has a paper veneer). Most of the papers are from the 1920's, much of which can still be read. Of particular interest is the grandfather clock which has newspapers from each of the (then) 48 states, and you can read them all down the front of the clock.

Despite being made out of paper the house was built with running water and electricity, but the roof has a shingle covering over the paper as protection from the elements. The house has been open for viewing since about 1942.

HAWAII VOLCANO HIKING TOURS
HC3, Box 10032 Keaau, Hawaii

This volcano tour covers the 11 mile loop around Crater Rim on the Kilauea Iki Trail where you will see ferns that grow to 30ft high. This Hawaiian hot spot has generated over 80 volcanoes that today form the Hawaiian Islands and stretch out 1,500 miles. You may have to venture 200 miles beneath the surface of the earth to locate the source of the indescribable heat that is generated. This hot spot is formed by magma (molten lava) coming through the tectonic plate and erupting more or less continuously for up to 70 million years to create the islands. It is said that the Hawaiian Islands move across the Pacific Ocean at about the speed your fingernails grow, meaning the life of a Hawaiian volcano is 5-10 million years before it sinks back to the sea floor.

Mount Kea is the largest of the Big Island's 5 shield volcanoes rising to 13,796ft and is also the most massive mountain on earth occupying an area of 10,000 cubic miles. Although it has not erupted for over 4,500 years it is still a sight to behold and is home to one of the largest astronomical bases in the world due to the superb high altitude viewing.

Kilauea is the youngest and most active volcano and has been erupting for over 20 years. In fact it is one of the most active volcanoes in the world and is certain to make your tour spectacular.

Hawaiian eruptions are mainly non-explosive as the high temperature of the magma (1,200C) when it reaches the surface makes it liquid.

An overhead view of one of the most active volcanoes in the world - Kilauea - which has been erupting for well over 20 years.

Spectacular lava flows in Hawaii.

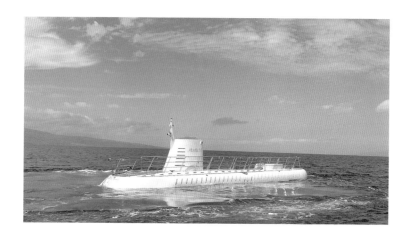

*Close up views
of marine life in
all its splendour
when you visit the
depths with
Atlantis Adventures,
the world's first
technologically advanced
passenger submarine.*

ATLANTIS ADVENTURES
75-5669 Alii Drive, Kailua-Kona, Hawaii

Equally as spectacular as the Hawaiian volcanoes is the journey undersea with Atlantis Submarines, the world's first and most technologically advanced passenger submarine. The Tour, which takes place in the Atlantis 48-passenger submarine, descends to over 100ft giving you the opportunity to see close up the many superb species of marine life including turtles, fish and coral. In addition there are sunken shipwrecks and other forms of artificial reef. At over 100ft in length, the spacious air-conditioned interior of Atlantis has large viewing ports and good seating providing an experience that you will remember

forever. Atlantis Tours also cover the Caribbean and have numerous tours to choose from.

Founded by Dennis Hurd with $250,000 development capital, the world's first tourist submarine began operating in Grand Cayman Island in 1986 and was highly successful. The prototype has since been improved upon and in 1987 the 48-passenger submarine was designed and built. Subsequent 48-passenger submarines were launched in Kona, Maui, and Oahu on the Hawaiian Islands, and in 1994 a 64-passenger submarine was constructed. Just before the turn of the century Atlantis expanded its operations into semi-submersible and island tours in addition to submarine tours.

THE WINCHESTER MYSTERY HOUSE
525 South Winchester Boulevard, San Jose, California

It was in 1884 that wealthy widow Sarah L. Winchester, heiress of the famous Winchester Rifle fortune, arrived in the Santa Clara Valley of California to begin a building project of such magnitude that it was to occupy her until her death some 38 years later. She purchased a 6 room house that was still under construction together with over 160 acres of surrounding land and, throwing away the blueprints, she began to build, and build . . . . and build. For 36 years with a dedicated team of craftsmen they built, altered, rebuilt, constructed, demolished, and then rebuilt again. About 2 dozen carpenters alone were kept working continually on the project and Sarah imposed her ideas and plans for the building throughout the years - strange though they were.

Known to be quite taken with the number '13' almost every staircase had 13 steps, many of the wooden floors contained 13 sections, the windows contained 13 panes of glass, the walls had 13 panels, and there are 13 bathrooms. Lining the driveway are 13 fan palm trees and it is even known that her will was divided into 13 parts and signed 13 times. Being spiritual in addition to superstitious a seance room in the centre of the house could be entered and left by numerous ways and it is believed she did this to confuse the spirits to whom she spoke to each night - ringing a bell to summon them. Sarah also slept in a different room each night as she believed the spirits were angry at the near completion of the house and it is this that convinced her that she would never complete the construction. Following her peaceful death aged 82 the house was sold by her niece to an investment group and is now a major tourist attraction.

Rare for its time, this Victorian mansion had gas lights that operated by the press of a button, 3 working elevators, and modern heating and sewerage systems. There are believed to be 160 rooms spread over almost 5 acres of land but the bizarre phenomena that gave the mansion its name is evident throughout. There are upside down posts, staircases that lead to nowhere, and even one that has 42 steps and turns 7 times (with each step only 2 inches high). Some doors lead into walls whilst one opens up to a drop of about 15ft into the garden below. There are windows in floors and numerous other astonishing features at The Winchester Mystery House.

The Winchester Firearms Museum has a superb collection, whilst the Winchester Antique Products Museum is a rare collection of antique products once manufactured by the Winchester Products Company. The Garden Tour is a must see boasting shrubs and flowers from all parts of the world and almost 14,000 miniature boxwood hedges. When Sarah was alive she had a full-time staff of 8 gardeners.

Declared a California Historical Landmark, The Winchester Mystery House has been visited hundreds of times by psychics since it has been open to the public. Many claim sightings or strange phenomena to report. In addition to this members of the public and staff have encountered mysterious voices, strange orbs of light, cold spots, and poltergeist experiences. Was Sarah L. Winchester trying to tell us something?

A small part of the famous Winchester Mystery House.

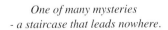

*One of many mysteries
- a staircase that leads nowhere.*

THE HOUSE ON THE ROCK

5754 Highway 23, Spring Green, Wisconsin

Its impossible to see everything the House on the Rock has to offer on a single visit. This is a place that will literally blow your mind, and no matter where you have travelled or what you have seen, the world over, you have never seen anything like this. The house is an architectural marvel perched on top of a 60ft chimney of rock in the Wyoming Valley. It was designed and built by Alex Jordan of Madison in the 1940's using over 5,000 tons of limestone and an equal amount of mortar. It is now a stupendous and extraordinary complex of rooms, gardens, streets and buildings, covering over 200 acres. The 14th room to be added, in 1985, is probably the most visually stunning and spectacular (not to say scariest) room you will ever walk into. Called the Infinity Room, it has 3,264 windows for walls and projects out an unsupported 218ft over the Wyoming Valley below. There is no other room in the world quite like it.

You approach the House on the Rock via a 375ft ramp through the treetops. Inside the Gate House entrance, waterfalls and massive fireplaces can be seen. There are thousands of things to be seen in the house. Space permits only a short description of some of the dazzling array of attractions, but amongst the best are an incredible collection of armour, a 4-storey high sea monster, a fully animated circus orchestra, and the world's largest carousel complete with over 20,000 lights, 269 real and mythical creatures, and weighing 35 tons. The greatest collection of animated, automated music machines and pipe organs in the world can be seen here in addition to the world's only mechanically operated symphony orchestra. Over a million pieces make up the collection of miniature circuses. Quite spectacular.

ROCK IN THE HOUSE

440 North Shore Drive, Fountain City, Wisconsin

From The House On The Rock to the Rock in the House. On April 24th, 1995, a 55 ton boulder rolled 400ft down a cliff and plowed into the 2-bedroom house of Dwight and Maxine Anderson, wedging itself into their home. The couple were rescued from the debris unhurt but moved out immediately for fear of another boulder hurtling down. They returned only to collect their belongings. A local real estate investor bought the house and turned it into a tourist attraction called the Rock in the House.

Does lightning strike twice? The garage at the side of the Anderson's home is where a house owned by the Dubler family once stood. One night in 1940 the elderly couple were asleep when tragedy struck. A giant stone came tumbling through the woods above the house and careered into the Dubler home. It was of such short duration they did not hear it and Mr Dubler woke to find himself dropped into the cellar amid the ruins of his home, practically uninjured. His wife however had been struck squarely by the rock as she lay on the outside of the bed. Her body was mangled beyond recognition.

WINDOW FOR VIEWING ONLY
NO ACCESS BEYOND THIS POINT

*Walking into the amazing Infinity Room
(top left) at The House on the Rock, and a
look down through a glass viewing panel in
the floor (top right). The Infinity Room juts
out an unsupported 218ft over the Wyoming
Valley (above) and has 3,264 windows
for walls.*

*The 55-ton boulder (right) that hurtled
400ft down a cliff to create the
'Rock in the House' at Fountain City.*

NEW ORLEANS CEMETERY & GRIS-GRIS WALKING TOUR

**All New Orleans Tours,
2634 Airport Drive,
Las Vegas, Nevada**

With over 650 different tours to choose from including travel by bus, helicopter, jeep, and even horseback, All New Orleans Tours is certain to have a themed tour to suit any taste. Perhaps the most bizarre tour on offer is the ghoulish New Orleans Cemetery & Gris-Gris Walking Tour. This is a one-of-kind walking tour of the most haunted cemetery in New Orleans - St.Louis No.1 Cemetery - which was featured in the movie 'Easy Rider' and is the final resting place of the notorious Voodoo Queen of New Orleans, Marie Leaveau.

The Tour is a unique opportunity to experience the spiritual side of New Orleans in addition to learning about the Voodoo spell casting method known as Gris-Gris (pronounced 'Gree-Gree'). You will also receive an authentic Gris-Gris bag, find out about the mysterious contents it contains, and visit the tomb of Marie Leaveau. The professional guide will also tell you about the strange above ground burial customs and the tombs of various 'societies'. Voodoo is still practiced in New Orleans today and there are many temples, museums and shops relating to this melting pot of religion and magic.

Widely acclaimed as America's most haunted city, New Orleans is also acknowledged as the birthplace of Voodoo in America following its spread from Haiti

in the wake of the Haitian slave revolt of 1791-1804. Voodoo is the Haitian folk religion consisting of African magical beliefs and rites mixed with certain Catholic elements. The African elements include the worship of the ancestral dead and loa (supernatural entities), together with dancing and the use of drums. Catholic elements include prayers, baptism, and the use of crosses, bells and candles. It began with the arrival of slaves in the New World and the subsequent suffering of blacks under impoverished, and merciless conditions. Most had nothing to cling to save their Gods and they were even prevented that as it was deemed 'heathen' beliefs. The majority of the slaves worshipped their Gods under the guise of worshipping Catholic saints.

Many legends and myths surround New Orleans most dominant Voodoo activist Marie Leaveau. She was believed to have been born of the spirits or sent as an envoy from the saints, although it is known she was the daughter of 'Sirene'. She sold potions and charms from her home during the 1830's, led Voodoo dances, and held ceremonies at which she was said to possess magical powers. One Voodoo rite she conducted on the banks of a river had naked dancing, animal sacrifices and bonfires, and is said to have resembled a scene from hell. She held a strange power over judges and the police, and was instrumental in saving numerous criminals from death by hanging.

Marie Leaveau died in 1881, aged 98, and is buried at St.Louis No.1 Cemetery. She is said to have looked 60 years younger. The inscription on the plaque placed on her tomb by the Catholic Church reads; 'this notorious Voodoo queen'.

HOLYLAND USA
1060 Jericho Road, Bedford, Virginia

Call it divine inspiration if you will but 250 acres and a replica and depiction of the life and deeds of Jesus Christ - in Virginia - takes a whole lot of inspiration. This nature sanctuary has been completely transformed into a reproduction of the Bible lands of Israel. Your 3 mile journey begins in Bethlehem where Jesus was born before heading north into Judean hill country to Shepherds Field where you can mingle with goats, donkeys and sheep. Following in the steps of Jesus you then go down the road to Jericho and venture into the Jordan Valley to the Galilee Country. In Nazareth you have time to explore Joseph's carpentry shop and a drink of water from Mary's well before crossing the Jordan River and skirting the Sea of Galilee to Capernaum. From there it is on to Samaria and eventually Jerusalem where the Dome of the Rock on Mount Moriah, the Synagogue, the 3 crosses on Mount Calvary, and the

empty tomb can be viewed. On to Bethany where Lazarus was raised from the dead and then to the famous Mount of Olives where Jesus ascended into Heaven. Phew! Numerous different tours - on foot, bus, van, even a hay wagon. Holy Land guide and gift shop also provided. Only in America!

MIAMI DUCK TOURS
1665 Washington Avenue, South Beach, Miami, Florida

Splash down into the water at Biscayne Bay for a real close up view of the homes of the seriously rich and famous who live on Star Island, on an amphibious vehicle operated by Miami Duck Tours. Resembling a plane without wings, the vehicles provide a great way to explore the magical City of Miami by road and water. The 90 minute fully narrated Land & Sea Adventure Tour explores the Art Deco District, Versace Mansion, the Port of Miami, Freedom Tower, Millionaire's Row, Star, Hibisucs and Palm Island, plus a whole lot more.

"Hold tight everyone. This is your driver . . . er, captain speaking".

CORAL CASTLE
28655 South Dixie Highway, Homestead, Florida

Edward Leedskalnin was born in Riga, Latvia, on August 10th, 1887, and when he arrived in America many years later, he had a dream to fulfill. He was heartbroken and devastated by the tragic loss of his one true love in life - Agnes, whom he referred to as his 'Sweet Sixteen' - and set out on a quest to create a monument to his lost love. When Ed was 26 he fell in love with Agnes and although she was 10 years younger than him he asked her to marry him. Agnes accepted but cancelled the wedding just a day before the ceremony was due to take place.

What makes this story quite remarkable is the fact that Ed was only 5ft tall and weighed just 100lbs.

Without any machinery or help, Ed created 'Coral Castle' (originally called the 'Rock Park Gate') out of over 1,200 tons of coral as a testimony to his lost love, Agnes.

Ed had moved to Florida in 1918 to benefit from the better climate, as he had developed tuberculosis. The original castle was built in Florida City and the coral that he worked on was up to 4,000ft thick. He carved and moved all of the coral without any assistance, moving huge blocks of it using only hand tools. The only skills he had acquired were from working on lumber camps in Latvia. Incredibly, each section of the walls of the castle were 8ft tall, 4ft wide, 3ft thick, and weighed over 58 tons. Some of the blocks used were twice the weight of the largest blocks in the Great Pyramid in Egypt. Primitive handmade tools were all that Ed had to create his masterpiece. He laboured continuosly for 28 years building this astonishing marvel.

All of the furniture within the Coral Castle is also made out of solid coral including a 20ft table and chairs (shown opposite page). A rocking chair weighs several ton's and could be rocked with the touch of a single finger.

Nearby building plans were set to interfere with Ed's work, and being a very private person Ed decided to pack up and move. In 1936 he bought 10 acres of land in Homestead and spent the next 3 years moving everything he'd made to this new location, where it remains today. How on earth Ed moved these giant carvings and enormous blocks a distance of 10 miles is still unknown today. He had a tractor and a battered old truck he had borrowed, as Ed only owned an old bicycle, but no-one saw Ed loading or unloading the truck. He did most of the work at night

by lantern, and there were numerous lookout posts along the castle walls to protect his privacy. When questioned about how he moved these gigantic blocks Ed would only say that he understood the laws of weight and leverage. His herculean efforts have baffled scientists and engineers and many have compared them to the construction of Stonehenge - or even the Pyramids. Perhaps the most astonishing monument to Ed's genius at Coral Castle is the 9 ton gate (shown opposite page) which he shaped and fashioned from a single piece of coral. Originally used as a turnstile, the gate fits within a quarter of an inch of the walls on either side and is carved with such perfect balance it used to open at the mere touch of a child's finger. These days it is braked open to prevent the 9 ton monster from swinging into people who are unaware of its movement. The gate has been the subject of many articles and publications who sought the answer to this seemingly impossible feat, then in 1986 the gate stopped opening. A team of engineers and a 50 ton crane revealed that the gigantic rock was centred on an old truck bearing. Ed had drilled a perfectly round hole from the top to the bottom of the 8ft high gate with no electric tools! Complete with new bearings and shaft the gate was replaced back into place later that year.

Sadly, in 1951, visitors saw a sign on the door of Ed's castle saying 'Going to the hospital'. Ed had become ill, taken a bus to Jackson Memorial Hospital in Miami, and died 3 days later in his sleep. He is said to have suffered malnutrition and kidney failure.

Harry, Ed's nephew and only living relative, inherited the Castle, and Ed's life savings of $3,500 were found there. Shortly before Harry himself died in 1953 he sold the property, which was then known as 'Rock Park Gate', to a Chicago family who subsequently renamed it Coral Castle. It is now on the National Register of Historic Places.

The Coral Castle is an everlasting mystery borne out of one man's unrequited love. Was it built using ancient sciences? When Hurricane Andrew struck in 1993 devastation lay outside Coral Castle, but all within was untouched. Billy Idol wrote his hit song 'Sweet Sixteen' about Ed's lost love, and a tour of Coral Castle makes you feel some of that sorrow. Somewhat ironically, the Castle can now be hired for weddings.

Enter, if you dare, through the mouth of a demon.

*The spooky
Haunted Monster Museum.*

PROFESSOR CLINE'S HAUNTED MONSTER MUSEUM
Natural Bridge, Virginia

Professor Cline's Haunted Monster Museum opened in 2002. It is set in a stone Victorian manor house that was previously called the Stonewall Inn and was constructed in 1870. This was used as a hunting lodge until the early 1970's when the Inn was closed.

You enter the Monster Museum through a creaky old gate that resembles the mouth of a demon and then proceed along the crumbling driveway through what is known as 'Freakout Forest'. Set back in the woods is an ogre eating a child, and a graveyard. This bizarre and unique haunted house style attraction - which is near the historic landmark, Natural Bridge of Virginia - is entered when you reach the top of the hill. A creepy organ booms out as you approach, and when you push the bell an hysterical voice tells you to 'get out before its too late'.

Full of chills and thrills this is a haunted house like many others, with zombies appearing from nowhere, flashing lights, and terrifying sounds. Where it comes out better than the others is in the authentic old house setting which is complete with ancient cobwebs and peeling paint.

Mark Cline, who opened this attraction, also designed 'Foamhenge'. His work has been seen in Alice Cooper's stage shows and on national television, and his skills in creating the very best spooky attractions can be seen throughout the USA.

VAMPIRE TOUR OF SAN FRANCISCO
Huntingdon Park, California, San Francisco

One of the best vampire tours you will experience is the Vampire Tour of San Francisco. On this tour you will explore the gothic side of Nob Hill, stopping off at numerous places whilst learning of their history and how Vampires played a part in that history.

Your host is Mina Harker, a vampress who was created by Count Dracula in London in 1897 and thereafter banished to exile in the United States. She has walked the streets of San Francisco for over 100 years now and is well qualified in relating to you the important part vampires have played in the shaping of San Francisco as it is today. The chilling script she narrates will have you knotting that scarf a little tighter round your neck before this hugely entertaining tour is even part of the way through.

Winner of several awards, the Vampire Tour of San Francisco is a great way to forget the weather, which can get mighty cold here. You are also invited to turn up in costume if you wish; Mina has traditional black vampire attire which she has worn for over 100 years.

DINOSAUR LAND
3848 Stonewall Jackson Highway, White Post, Virginia

Replicas of the giants that once roamed the earth can be seen at this roadside attraction that is almost as old as them. From the awesome meat eaters to the gigantic grazers, they are all here in splendid fibreglass glory. That's not to say the scare you'd get on a cold windswept winter morning, from a 90ft monster, would be mild. Far from it as these are some of the best reproductions you are ever likely to see. There are no moving parts or flashy gimmicks here, just monsters of the past to trigger your imagination as you step through the cave-like entrance. There are about 30 dinosaurs represented here together with an assortment of other beasts. If an epic battle between Tyrannosaurus (above) and Titanosaurus or a fearsome Megalosaurus fails to stir you, then your glasses may be misted over.

Fearsome giants galore at Dinosaur Land in Virginia.

GRANDMA PRISBREY'S BOTTLE VILLAGE
Simi Valley, California

In 1956, at the age of 60, Tressa 'Grandma' Prisbrey set out to transform her property and land into Bottle Village. It began simply as a practical need for inexpensive building materials to construct a wall to keep away the fumes and dirt from the nearby turkey farm, and to build a structure to house her collection of 17,000 pencils. An avid collector, she also had a shell collection and a huge collection of dolls from around the world. However, Grandma Prisbrey enjoyed her new found fun and creativity so much that over the next 25 years Bottle Village was to take over her life; tens of thousands of bottles were crafted into numerous buildings, wishing wells, walkways, shrines, and any other number of random constructions. Many of her idiosyncratic creations defied belief. The Dolls Head Shrine and car headlights constructions were bizarre to say the least.

For years and years she built, the majority of the bottles used being unearthed at the local dump. Amber beer bottles were placed in horizontal rows, thousands of clear bottles were painted inside, and blue Milk of Magnesia bottles were a particular favourite for many creations. She offered walking tours to anyone who was interested taking them room by room along mosaic walks, and amusing them with old stories. These tours would always end in the meditation room where she would play the piano and sing 1920's songs.

Grandma Prisbrey died in 1988 but Bottle Village, having been partly destroyed by the Northridge earthquake, is still there as a personal statement to the importance of creativity. Some say that Grandma Prisbrey's prescence lingers on, and the many religious structures, wishing wells, and references to maternity and magic throughout her Village make you wonder. Her life was certainly not without difficulties. She married her first husband when she was only 15 and he was 52, having 7 children by him. She subsequently left him and raised all of the children herself. Death struck 6 of her 7 children during her lifetime and it seems that Bottle Village was her personal approach to converting sorrow into creativeness.

What is left of the once amazing Dolls Head Shrine at Bottle Village. This was one of many odd creations that Grandma Prisbrey found time to make during the 25 year period she constructed the Village.

GATORLAND
14501 South Orange Blossom Trail, Orlando, Florida

Located in Florida, which is known as the Alligator Capital of the World, is Gatorland - a 110 acre alligator theme park and wildlife preserve. At the 800 seater arena tourists are left guessing which one out of a dozen or more of these prehistoric beasts is next to be wrestled. The spectacle is amazing as gator 'wranglers' climb on the back of a snapping 8ft alligator whilst pointing out survival features to the audience. The 'Gator Jumparoo' Show is similar in thrills as you watch some of the largest alligators in the world actually jump 5ft out of the water to clamp their powerful jaws around a dangling chicken carcass. These ferocious predators put on an awesome display of sheer power and strength for the watching crowd.

Other attractions at Gatorland, which opened in 1949, include 'Jungle Crocs', and 'Upclose Encounters' where you meet fascinating creatures from around the world including some of the most dangerous snakes there are.

Alligators and crocodiles are similar in appearance but differ in a few ways. When an alligator's mouth is closed you can see its teeth, and it's snout is also shorter and rounder than a crocodile's. Alligators have rows of scales on their body and live near water as they are cold-blooded (to maintain body temperature). They will also dig into mud to hibernate during cold winters.

Gatorland welcomes you (above) and (right) the show goes on with a frenzy of feeding.

DEARLY DEPARTED TOURS
5419 Hollywood Boulevard, Hollywood, California

Travel through decades of death and murder as you are escorted to famous and infamous locations throughout Los Angeles in the luxurious comfort of the Dearly Departed Tomb Buggy. What next you may think, but this is a tour like no other and your guide knows where the bodies are buried!

Covering almost 3 hours, you will be shown where the notorious Manson murders occurred, the assassination spot of Bobby Kennedy, the real Nightmare on Elm Street (the Menendez home), and the final destinations of greats such as Bela Lugosi, Frank Sinatra, River Phoenix, and many more. In all there are almost 100 sites featured on this tour making it great value for money, if a little gruesome.

BULLDOG TOURS GHOST & GRAVEYARD TOUR
40 North Market Street, Charleston, South Carolina

Hear about the infamous individuals who found their final resting place in the Holy City on the Ghost & Graveyard tour operated by Bulldog Tours. It is one of a number of trips they run themed on the 'dark side' but it is the most atmospheric and spooky.

The night tour of Charleston Cemetery, one of the oldest graveyards in the country, will frighten but also intrigue as you inspect the headstones and step across the graves. This is a tour that dares to go where others won't and will leave you wondering why us mere mortals subject ourselves to this kind of punishment.

Charleston Cemetery - not so terrifying by day.

ZERO GRAVITY CORPORATION
4101 Ravenswood Road, Dania Beach, Florida

Zero-G was formed in the mid 1990's, although it was initially conceived in the early 1990's. The initial focus was in choosing the Boeing 727-200 aircraft as the airframe of choice. This was then followed by painstaking engineering tests to demonstrate the safety aspect of the airplane for parabolic flights, and the company gained its first experimental license in 2000.

Fully operational now, Zero-G offer weightless flight (which is also known as parabolic flight) aboard their Boeing 727 aircraft named G-Force One. Weightlessness is achieved through a parabolic flight manoeuver between 24,000 and 34,000ft altitude, with each parabola taking 10 miles of airspace to perform and lasting about a minute from start to finish. The exhilarating experience, previously only available to trainee NASA astronauts, is the thrill of a lifetime and is the closest you can get to walking on Mars or the Moon.

The manoeuver has been likened to a roller coaster as the plane is initially pulled up to a 45 degrees 'nose high'. Next the plane is 'pushed over' the top to reach the zero-gravity segment of the parabolas. For the next 25-30 seconds everything in the plane is weightless. At approximately 30 degrees 'nose low' a gentle pull-out is started which allows passengers to stabilize on the aircraft floor. The manoeuver is then repeated and the weightlessness experienced is equivalent to the type of 'free fall' experienced when sky diving. Buzz Aldrin (the Apollo 11 Astronaut) remarked, "It was exhilarating; it was great to experience both Lunar gravity and weightlessness again. I hope that everyone interested in adventure tourism and space will participate in this amazing opportunity".

All flights are fully insured, have an impeccable safety record, and feature approximately 15 parabolas which lasts about 90 to 100 minutes. So if you want to feel like Superman you can fly the entire length of the airplane. Hope there's no Kryptonite aboard.

How to lose weight without dieting - aboard Zero-G.

CABELA'S
100 Cabela Drive, Hamburg, Pennsylvania

Cabela's promote themselves as being the 'World's Foremost Outfitter of hunting, fishing and outdoor gear'. In 1961, Dick Cabela decided to sell fishing flies he had purchased whilst at a furniture show in Chicago. After a couple of attempts at newspaper advertising, some of which included free introductory offers, he soon had orders arriving from sportsmen and women around the country. Other lines were added to the mail order operation and it soon grew. By 1964 bigger premises were needed, and the basement of his father's furniture store was used. In 1969 Cabela's was operating in a 50,000 sq.ft building in Sydney, Nebraska, and today, Cabela's have a state-of-the-art World headquarters, numerous stores throughout the USA, and they mail out more than 120 million catalogues to all 50 states and more than 120 countries.

This colossal 250,000 sq.ft, Hamburg, Pensylvania, store is like all others and specialises in hunting equipment and outdoor merchandise. They also have entertainment attractions featuring massive taxidermy displays of museum quality animals in realistic settings akin to their natural habitats. Take the tour of a store, and you feel you've been transported to a Tarzan film location. The Hamburg store has a green edifice and huge parking lot. As with other Cabela's, Conservation Mountain is the main exhibit, and you could spend an hour or more walking around this and admiring the wildlife which includes bears mauling a moose, and other animal savagery scenes depicted. Why its called Conservation Mountain is anyone's guess.

Deer Country is another huge exhibit, complete with foliage and woodland setting, whilst The African Diorama is a chunk of the Serengeti brought to vivid realism; a pride of lions hunt down their prey, and a couple of alligators rip apart a wildebeest - such is the survival of the fittest. Numerous other large exhibits are to be seen throughout the store.

In keeping with the 'big-is-best' American attitude, there is a 55,000 gallon tank of fish here, and even a super-sized Gun Library which is packed-out with customers within an hour of the store opening. Camouflage for the serious hunter is big here, if you can find it. Seriously, there are rows and rows of outfits, many of which can transform you into an innocuous bush or even a tree. Cabela's also encourage hunters to donate their own trophy mounts for display in their stores.

Core values - as pointed out on their website - include quality products and services, excellence in performance, and respect for individuals. Not much of that respect went to the hundreds of dead animals that gaze back at you with glassy eyes in a Cabela's store. A visit is certainly one that youngsters will be enthralled by, but a thought provoking experience for many adults. A part of you is left thinking that animals are meant to be seen alive and kicking in their own world, or even a zoo. Is there really a need for legions of stuffed animals to assist the tills ringing in the 'World's Foremost Outfitter of hunting, fishing and outdoor gear'?

CRYSTAL CATHEDRAL
12141 Lewis Street,
Garden Grove, California

With only $500 in his pocket and nothing but a dream to inspire him Rev. Robert H.Schuller and his wife Arvella arrived in Southern California in 1955. His dream was to build a great church for God, one that would change and save lives. Over 50 years later his dream had become reality with the majestic building known as the Crystal Cathedral, the largest glass structured building in the world. It resembles a 4-pointed star and consists of over 10,000 panes of glass forming the translucent walls. The chapel in the cathedral tower has a quite stunning glass cross. Located in Garden Grove, California, the Crystal Cathedral is now the home base for the International Cathedral Ministries, has a congregation of over 10,000 members, and has a televised 'Hour of Power' show that is broadcast live across the nation and regularly features the obligatory celebrity guest.

The Crystal Cathedral campus is where thousands of people communicate daily with issues of faith, mind and soul, and the Crystal Cathedral promises something for everyone - especially you!

Now that TV evangelist Schuller has his dream he is building on it. Guided tours are held every half hour throughout the week, such is the popularity of this glazier's paradise He is also the author of more than 30 books, many of which have appeared on the New York Times bestseller list. There is obviously money as well as belief in faith. Praise the Lord.

Crystal Cathedral,
the largest glass structured
building in the world.

HOEGH PET CASKET COMPANY
Delta Avenue, Gladstone, Michigan

There are strange tours and there are bizarre tours but the strangest bizarre tour is the Hoegh Pet Casket Company Tour. Said to be a pioneer of pet caskets (animal coffins to us), Hoegh Industries has been producing these vacuum formed plastic burial shells since 1966 and has sold well over a million by now. They are sold in approximately 8 sizes and about 25 different styles, with cremation urns and remembrance plaques also being popular sellers. In fact they ship to hundreds of locations in the USA every week in addition to overseas orders from Australia, Japan, England, and most other countries.

The showroom is a mournful place with candles, floral arrangements, and pictures of animals, although it is not known whether they were previous customers or not (sort of rover's return if they were). Your tour continues with the opportunity to learn about the caskets that make most sales, viewing a video in the conference room explaining Pet Cemetery theory, and seeing the vacuform machine where the casket interiors are made. The warehouse is regularly filled with heaps of casket shells and other finished products, like a pet's armageddon.

The tours are all done tongue-in-cheek in a jovial and good natured atmosphere and if you cant afford the casket of your dreams there's always that tupperware box at the back of your kitchen cupboard at home.

SAN FRANCISCO ZOO VALENTINE'S DAY SEX TOURS
San Francisco Zoo, 1 Zoo Road, San Francisco, California

This reservation-only attraction (limited to adults) held several days each February at San Francisco Zoo takes up to 100 people on a tour of fornicating felines, and monkeys monkeying about. It is pure coincidence that the San Francisco Zoo Valentine's Day Sex Tours appears on page 69 of this guide.

Started in 1989, the tour's popularity has seen it become an annual event. Everything from alligator sex, gay penguins, and opossums that can get pregnant when they are pregnant (as they have double wombs) is covered. Tapirs are said to be some of the zoo's better endowed animals (elephants excepted), whilst a lion can have sex up to 40 times within 24 hours - albeit in 30-second chunks. To see a rhino having sex is a spectacle in itself as it is extremely violent and they can be locked together for hours.

So the bears bare their bums and the tiger tends his tackle. A very interesting 4-hour tour which includes a ride on the jungle love train, but San Francisco is a long way to go just to see God's creatures cavorting when 'Animal Farm' can probably be downloaded for free off the internet.

VIOLENT SKIES TOURS
7633 E.63rd Place, Memorial Place, Suite 3002, Tulsa, Oklahoma
UK Office - 3 Shenstone Court, Forge Lane, Halesowen, West Midlands
Tel: 0121 585 8559

The power of nature is truly awe-inspiring and some of nature's most stunning events take place over the Central Plains of the USA. Storm chasing is big business in the States and the myriad of companies seeking your business makes it difficult to choose the right option. Violent Skies Tours are one of the very best specialists in storm chasing tours

offering a choice of Tornado, Water Spout, or Quickflight Hurricane Chase themed tours. Breathtaking views, stunning scenery, and the thrill of the chase make any of these tours the experience of a lifetime.

The very latest equipment in storm chasing technology is used to pinpoint and track severe storms. Technology plays a key role in severe weather forecasting and experts will ensure your trip is unforgettable. A computer

system is in use that integrates with the chasing equipment, flat panel touch screens display all the data, and high-resolution monitors are in the front and back of each vehicle to allow every

person to watch. A host of other technical equipment is in use including GPS tracking systems.

The famous Tornado Alley provides the setting for the Tornado Tours during the storm season where you hunt down thunderstorms and tornadoes. The Water Spout Tours seek out rotating columns of air which have formed over the warm oceans during unstable atmospheric conditions. Quickflight Hurricane Chase Tours whisk you off to the nearest major airport near the targeted area of a land falling hurricane. When a hurricane is approximately 48-72 hours from land fall, Violent Skies will collect you at a pre-designated airport to transport you to the carefully selected area for intercepting the hurricane. Beats watching television any day.

VIC'S GOLD PANNING
Hwy 119, south of Black Hawk, Colorado

There's gold in them thar hills . . . or so we hope on a visit to Vic's Gold Panning. Bring your own equipment or use their gold pans - whatever you choose its a great day out with a difference for all the family. Established in 1957, Vic's Gold Panning was featured in National Geographic Magazine in 1969 and has been going strong ever since. It is one of several 'pay-to-pan' sites in Colorado, and they offer expert tuition on how to pan for gold using modern equipment.

Of course there are strict guidelines governing gold panning at Vic's. Somewhat tongue-in-cheek their code of conduct includes never digging within 15ft of another prospector's diggings - unless invited, and always refill your holes and replace vegetation that was disturbed (apparently required by law). Other quaint rules include avoiding prospecting in spawning trout water during the spawning season, and never refuel or oil any equipment in or near water (also the law). Their most bizarre advice is 'if you've packed it in . . pack it out. Do not litter, and if you find litter some fart smeller left behind then please take it with you'.

Vic's invite you to 'bring the lil' ol' woman along for the fun - otherwise they might moan and groan all week long'. On a more serious note this really is a fun day out, though who knows what might happen if you unearth a giant golden nugget.

Gold discovered at Vic's, and a summer shot of part of the site.

ELMIRA BIGFOOT SEARCH TOURS
Strathmont Plaza, 100 North Main Street, Elmira, New York

The legend of Bigfoot has been around a long time. Also known as the 'Sasquatch' or the 'missing link', Bigfoot roams around isolated areas of the Northwest United States and Western Canada. Descriptions of the creature vary but most are similar to those of the Abominable Snowman, or Yeti, of the Himalayas. Described as primate in

Bigfoot - man or beast?

appearance, the beast has thick hair covering every part of the body except his face and hands and is said to be half-man, half-monkey. He is rumoured to walk silently and upright, emits a high-pitched cry when disturbed, and sightings put him at anything between

6ft and 12ft in height. One of the world's greatest unexplained cryptozoological mysteries, the remarkable fact is that with almost every sighting researchers and other witnesses have found giant footprints at the scene - mostly twice the size of an average adult human footprint. The many thousands of reported sightings each year have led people to believe there is more than one Bigfoot, and therefore there must be males and females of the species.

The most notable of all Bigfoot sightings happened in an unpopulated mountain valley near the California and Oregon border in 1967. The footage taken at the time is now world famous and clearly shows a huge hairy manlike creature running through a clearance. A still taken from this footage (known as the Patterson footage) is shown opposite.

Whatever the truth is behind the Bigfoot phenomenon there is no doubt it is big news in the USA. There are numerous companies offering tours that cover from a single day to a fully inclusive camping week. The Elmira Bigfoot Search Tours are said to be one of the best as their trips venture into some of the 'hotspots' for sightings of this mysterious creature. They also offer inclusive meals and insurance on their tour packages. No camping or hiking experience is required and your tour consists of several searches deep in the woods where a couple of Bigfoot are believed to be living in a large cave. They are rumoured to be frequently active around camping sites on the hill. As Sherlock Holmes said to Dr. Watson; "there's something's afoot my dear Watson".

Part Three
- REST OF WORLD -

Puzzling World, where things may
not be what they seem - page 87.

THE PHARAONIC VILLAGE
3 Al-bahr El Aazam, Jacob Island, Giza, Egypt

You step back in time; approximately 3,000 years, when you go on a fantastic journey of discovery at The Pharaonic Village. Brought to life by an amazing group of well over 100 actors and actresses, visitors will find exact reproductions of buildings, monuments, clothing, and even lifestyles at this most precise recreation of Pharaonic Egypt. This educational theme park has motorised barges which leisurely work their way through a network of canals whilst you see re-enactments of life in ancient Egypt; farmers, weavers, boat builders, and all kinds of other representations of daily Egyptian life. Some of the areas can also be walked through.

Although close to the heart of Cairo the Pharaonic Village seems a world away as it is surrounded by trees. Of great interest is the replica of Tutankhamun's tomb which has copies of all the objects found when the tomb was discovered. The contents of the entire tomb have been reproduced using the same techniques used in ancient times, and following Howard Carter's notes and original photographs.

A white stone Egyptian temple with a sacred lake is quite stunning, whilst there is even a military camp, marketplace, pharaoh's palace, and workers dwellings. No attention to detail has been spared throughout and this is a must-visit attraction for any visitor to Egypt that will complement your trip after seeing historical Luxor and Aswan.

The Pharaonic Village was an idea conceived by Dr.Hassan Ragab, famous for his rediscovery of the ancient techniques for making papyrus. He founded the Dr.Ragab Papyrus Institute in Cairo where you can see how the writing material is made and, in 1974, subsequently re-invested his profits into the reproduction of ancient Egyptian life on Jacob Island which opened to the public in 1984.

He began by planting over 5,000 trees to block the view of Cairo that surrounds the island, and scoured the world for plants and birds that had once been commonplace in ancient Egypt. Date palms and sycamores, and all types of roots and plants that had once flourished in Egypt thousands of years ago (and were depicted in tomb paintings as part of ancient Egyptian life) found their way to Jacob Island. Some could no longer be found in Egypt, some were extinct, but it mattered not to Dr.Ragab and he was not discouraged. He travelled the world in his quest for perfection and eventually a collection of plants and animals not seen in Egypt for many centuries found their home in The Pharaonic Village. Another quest then began to find out exact information on the daily life of ancient Egyptians. He visited museums and universities all over the world to gain this knowledge wanting to know every minute detail.

Over 10 years of work and $6 million were lavished on his project but even after opening to the public he continued to improve upon it. Today there are 9 or 10 museums and a plethora of Pharaonic related reproductions - each made in exacting detail.

The Pharonic Village at Jacob Island near Cairo where a re-enactment of ancient Egyptian life from 3,000 years ago can be seen.

*The beauty, splendour, and raw power
of the world's most famous waterfall.*

NIAGARA FALLS IMAX THEATRE & DAREDEVIL GALLERY

**6170 Fallsview Boulevard,
Niagara Falls, Ontario, Canada**

Niagara Falls is the most famous waterfall in the world. It actually consists of 3 falls; the American Falls and Bridal Veil Falls (also known as the Luna Falls) which are both in the USA, and the Horseshoe Falls which is in Canada. Its watercourse is the Niagara River. Famous for the many daredevils who have taken the plunge over the Falls, no visit to Niagara would be complete without experiencing the thrill of these thundering falls and their fascinating 12,000 year history at the Niagara Falls Imax Theatre & Daredevil Gallery. The Theatre is the home of one of the most spectacular adventures of all time - The Niagara Falls Movie. Hold onto your seats as this powerful film experience brings reality to life on a gigantic screen accompanied by 12,000 watts of earth shaking surround sound. The Daredevil gallery exhibition has a huge collection of Daredevil barrels and other contraptions which the adventurous (or foolhardy) have ventured over on, plus related memorabilia.

Whilst there are taller and larger waterfalls to be seen throughout the world it is Niagara Falls that is by far the most popular answer when asking the question of naming a famous waterfall. The Falls actually straddle the United States - Canadian International Border and are in both the State of New York and the Province of Ontario. The word 'Niagara' is derived from the Indian word 'Onguiaahra'

meaning 'the strait', and the Niagara River itself is actually a legacy of the last Ice Age when, 18,000 years ago, massive ice sheets carved out the basins of the Great Lakes. The mighty river plunges over the Falls then travels 15 miles or so until it reaches the Great Lake Ontario, and whilst the enormous volume of water never stops flowing, it did on 2 occasions stop completely; on 29th March 1848, due to an ice blockage in the upper part of the river, the flow was stopped to the point where people could actually walk out and pick up lost artifacts from the riverbed. Then in 1969 the American Falls was stopped for several months for a feasibility study to remove loose rock at the base.

Many people have lost their lives trying to conquer the Falls. As recent as 1995 Robert Overcracker rode a jetski over the Horseshoe Falls but his parachute did not open. He plunged to his death and his body was never recovered. In 1995 a man and woman became the first male and female to make the drop together, whilst in 2003 Kirk Jones became the first person to survive the drop wearing only the clothes on his back.

Niagara Falls is most famous for the countless people who have taken the plunge in assorted barrels. In 1901 Annie Taylor became the first person to actually conquer the Falls in a barrel, which was airtight and air pressured to 30 p.s.i. with a bicycle pump! The infamous Bobby Leach hurtled over in a steel barrel in 1911 and broke his jaw and both kneecaps, and in 1928 Jean Lussier survived the drop in a large rubber ball. There have been many more attempts and many to surely follow, such is the magnetism of Niagara Falls.

VISITE DES EGOUTS DE PARIS
Pont de l'Alma, Paris, France

Probably the most comprehensive sewer tour in the world with your friendly Parisiens guiding you around - and narrating the history - of the murky 2,000 km system, whilst you hop over channels with rivers of real 'floaters'.

MUSEE DES EGOUTS
Toll House, Porte d Anderlecht, Brussels, Belgium

An underground river that used to be an open sewer running through the city is the highlight of your Brussels Sewer Tour. These days its hidden from public view but still takes thousands of tons of raw sewage to be unceremoniously dumped in the North Sea.

The multilingual tours are good value for money if 'poo' is your chosen subject and the museum has loads of curious exhibits on display, all labelled in different languages.

EMPEROR'S BATHS - KAISERTHERMEN
Trier, Germany

Trier was once the capital of the Western Roman Empire, and the Emperor's Baths (Kaiserthermen), dating back to the 4th century, have dank and mysterious underground

passages which were once part of the ancient sewer network. An ideal location for historical turd photography.

FOREIGN VISITORS SEWER GALLERY - CIZINECK VSTUP DO KANALIZACE POD ORLOJEM
Old Town Hall, Prague, Czech Republic

This was built in 1906 when it was the most modern sewer system in the Austro-Hungarian Empire. It attracts a few foreign visitors but also many older residents of Prague who pop in from time to time to reminisce. Perhaps they feel a part of them has been this way before.

ANCIENT ROMAN SEWERS - CLOACA MAXIMA
Roman Forum (Foro Romano), Rome, Italy

Cloaca Maxima is the world's oldest functioning sewer dating back over 2,500 years. It can be viewed from several good vantage spots which not only illustrate how the system operates, but also how it continues to work with almost no maintenance.

UNREALDIVE
Kleinbaii Harbour, Gansbaii, South Africa

Shark Alley is a narrow channel between the islands of Geyser Rock and Dyer Island and is reputed to be the best place in the world for Great White shark cage diving. In fact it is known as 'the shark supermarket' because of the many resident seal colonies in the area. Only a short journey by boat from Gansbaii, Shark Alley is a perfect place to experience the thrills of meeting Great Whites face to face. No diving experience or qualifications are necessary as your cage dive takes place only metres below the surface of the water, but will leave you with memories that will last a lifetime. There is also no limit to the amount of time you can spend in the cage - although some may want to come up sooner rather than later.

When you reach your destination from Kleinbaii Harbour the Skipper will begin 'chumming', which is baiting the sharks to lure them in. You have the opportunity to take a cage dive as the sharks appear or alternatively watch from the deck of the boat for those of a nervous disposition. Your experience can also be shown to family and friends as the crew can video your dive for you.

UnrealDive also offer tailor-made diving trips for individuals and smaller groups and guarantee close proximity to some of the best diving, whale watching, and white shark viewing available anywhere in the world.

PANMUNJOM & DMZ TOUR
Panmunjom Co-Op Centre, Lotte Hotel, Sogongdong, Chung-Gu, Seoul, Korea

There's not really much to see or do at the DMZ (demilitarized zone) which is the no-man's land between North and South Korea, said to be the world's most heavily fortified border. There is a small museum, gift shop, a below ground tour of the 'Third Infiltration Tunnel' on the North side which would have allowed 10,000 soldiers an hour to cross into the South, and of course the coin-in-slot binoculars which permit close-up views of fur-hatted soldiers patrolling the DMZ. The real thrill comes from the tension in the air and an atmosphere that you could literally 'cut with a knife'. It is for this reason that busloads of tourists make the trip every day, and the history of the intense rivalry between these 2 sides certainly makes it worthwhile.

Strict rules operate regarding conduct, age, and clothing regulations on these tours. You are instructed not to pull faces or gesture to the North Korean soldiers or else! Although said to be at a standoff, North Korea's secretive nuclear bomb program can be very much in visitors minds when these tour guidelines are explained. An uneasy peace seems to have prevailed in recent years but the danger is still there. Onc look at the stone-faced guards makes you really feel North Korea's determination to invade the South, and in fact the majority of North Korea's 1.3 million army is deployed just north of this 2.5 mile wide strip of mines and barbed wire.

The DMZ Tour leaves more questions unanswered than answered and leaves plenty to ponder over whilst you check out your 'Joint-Security Area' t-shirt and souvenir plastic binoculars on the bus back.

FANTASEA TOURS
5 Albuoy's Point,
Hamilton HM11, Bermuda

The Bermuda Triangle - the mere mention of the name conjures up images of spectral ghost-ships, lost flights and unexplained mysteries. The area has claimed the lives of countless plane and ship passengers alike including those of Flight 19, which is perhaps the most famous aviation mystery in history after disappearing following a routine training mission off Florida in 1945. The most famous ship connected with these waters would be the Mary Celeste (1892) which was found drifting aimlessly within the Triangle without a living crew member aboard.

Situated in the western Atlantic Ocean the Triangle is so called by drawing a line between Bermuda, Fort Lauderdale (Florida), and Puerto Rico. This expanse of ocean is over a million square miles and has the 30,000 ft deep Puerto Rico Trench at its depths. Strange magnetic fields, alien abductions, lights in the sky, and monsters from the deep have all been blamed for the disappearances here, yet people are still drawn to visit the centre of what has also been called the 'Devil's Triangle'.

One of Fantasea Tours many exciting trips is a night time cruise into the notorious Bermuda Triangle in a glass bottomed boat. The ocean beneath you will suddenly be flooded with light as the boats underwater lights illuminate the depths. Dare you look? Will you disappear?

The 'Hall of Following Faces' at Puzzling World where huge reproductions of famous faces appear to follow you around the room and (below) an illusion room where your eyes will deceive you.

STUART LANDSBOROUGH'S PUZZLING WORLD
Main Highway, Wanaka, South Island, New Zealand

This attraction is located near Lake Wanaka on New Zealand's South Island, with Wanaka itself surrounded by the impressive Southern Alps and boasting several international quality ski resorts. The moment you approach The Puzzling World of Stuart Landsborough you realise it is something quite special as you cannot fail to see the bizarre and eccentric buildings - a leaning tower clock is a landmark that stands out even from some distance.

There is so much to see, do, and investigate here, with everything certain to amaze you. The 'Illusion Rooms' have to be seen to be believed - when entering you will pass through the 'Hologram Hall', which is noted for being one of the finest displays of creative holograms in the world. Then there is the 'Hall of Following Faces' where almost 200 enormous models of famous faces seem to follow you around the room. This is world unique, as is the 'Ames Forced Perspective Room', the technique of which was used in the Lord of the Rings film to create the illusion of little and tall people. The appearance of this room is totally distorted yet viewed through a window

outside it appears normal. The 'Haunted Illusion Room' is tilted at an angle of 15 degrees and when you enter it your brain is convinced it cannot be sloping, yet all the displays appear to be hanging at impossible angles.

The Great Maze (Labyrinth) is an incredible puzzle that was created by Stuart Landsborough in 1973 and was the forerunner of the world's modern style mazes (or labyrinths). The aim is to visit each of the 4 coloured corner towers before making it to the exit. A real challenge this one. Even the toilets at Puzzling World generate startled expressions on visitors faces, but we won't spoil the surprise so you'll have to visit. The cafe has numerous different puzzles on the table tops which can keep even ardent puzzle solvers at it for hours.

OCEAN DOME SEAGAIA
Kyushu Island, Miyazaki, Japan

You can see the real Pacific Ocean from the third floor tier of eating houses here. It is only 300 metres away from Ocean Dome Seagaia, so why build the world's largest indoor water park that near? Well, this is Japan, the land of the Rising Sun and home of technology and creation, so why not!

Seagaia (a combination of the words 'sea' which is English and 'gaia' which is Greek for earth) is a gigantic resort complex located on Kyushu Island on the Hitotsuba Coast of Japan's Miyazaki Prefecture. It stretches 6.2 miles from north to south and covers an area of 1,730 acres. The dome of Seagaia is retractable and encloses a man-made ocean complete with waves, beach, and a hot 30 degrees temperature which is maintained all year round. It can also accommodate a staggering 10,000 people. Inside the dome there are raft rides, tropical plants, water cascades, and a host of other aquatic attractions. During darkness a water screen creates striking lighting effects as laser lights patrol the artificial sea.

The heated ocean has a width of 140 metres and sends 13,500 tons of salt-free water cascading along 600 tons of polished marble chips that constitute the long shoreline that is fringed by a variety of shops. In this watery wonderland you may see American fashioned beach-boy Japanese surfers whizzing along on large artificial waves, which in turn are created on the world's largest artificial ocean. Great.

Fake palm trees, mechanised parrots, and a half-hourly mock volcanic eruption from Mount Bali Hai has not detracted from the immense enjoyment of the millions of visitors this resort has attracted since its grand opening in 1993. The complex itself is so vast it also houses restaurants, hotels, a wildlife park, golf, and other sporting activities. The high price paid to create this pre-packaged holiday of the future was 2 billion US dollars which puts the standard couple of hundred pounds a week beach-rakers wage at your typical British seaside resort into perspective.

Customers at Seagaia pay a single price for admission, which is not cheap, and further costs are deducted from a bar-coded tag you secure to your wrist. Dozens of shops offer everything from souvenirs to beach clobber, and sun lotion to a choice of cuisine. There are also festivals, music and dancing, and many special themed events.

You have to admire the Japanese for their invention and Seagaia is certainly a spectacular spectacle, although not quite the 8th wonder of the world. Fortunately, traditional sand and sea lovers still have numerous other options.

The huge Ocean Dome Seagaia complex with the real ocean to the left of the picture (above) and (below) inside Ocean Dome, a seaside playground of immense propertions.

MINIMUNDUS
Villacher Strabe, 9020
Klagenfurt, Carinthia, Austria

Plenty of model villages about but certainly nothing like this - Minimundus - over 150 miniatures of the most beautiful buildings from all 5 continents. Started in 1958 on a small scale (sic) the models have now become so realistic that many visitors come back time and again. Close attention is given to even the smallest detail by the expert model makers when making the exhibits with all original materials being used such as marble, basalt, sandstone, etc. With new models continually being added it is little

wonder that this is one of Austria's top visitor attractions.

This huge site also has much more for the visitor such as special landscapes and floral displays, 3D walks through the interiors of models, original sound documentation, and a space shuttle which 'blasts off' every hour. Many of the models are set against a backdrop representing the natural surroundings of the original building or structure with parts of Minimundus having been turned into desert landscapes and even a tropical rainforest. Visually stunning, don't forget your camera; if you stand close enough you can tell everyone you've been to all parts of the world and seen the lot!

DINOSAUR PROVINCIAL PARK
Patricia, Alberta, Canada

Dinosaur Provincial Park is located in the world famous, awe-inspiring badlands, a 2 hour drive east of Calgary where the prairie grasslands suddenly disappear and you enter a new world of 'pinnacles', 'coulees', and 'hoodoos'. In fact the visitor could believe they have been transported to another planet as strange land formations rise up all around you and it would appear that everything had suddenly turned to sandstone. The stunningly beautiful shapes that have been carved by wind and water are reminiscent of a moon landscape and there are many tricks played on the eye by these sometimes human and animal looking shaped figures.

Mysterious 'hoodoo'.

A trip to Dinosaur Provincial Park is also a trip back in time - 75 million years back in time to be exact. This region was then subtropical and was covered by a lush vegetation. Dinosaurs hunted here and the area today is one of the most stunningly rich fossil fields in the world. Such is the density of bone saturation here that it is highly probable you could yourself unearth the latest discovery!

The Park also provides a wide variety of services and facilities such as campsites, exhibits, hikes, and tours. The badlands bus tour will show you dinosaur remains and hugely impressive landforms, whilst the Centrosaurus Bone Bed Hike (one of the most exciting dinosaur excavation discoveries from the 1980's) will illustrate what is significant about a bed of bones that covers an area the size of 2 tennis courts. Other interesting trips include the Fossil Safari Hike, Camel's End Coulee Hike, and the Great Badlands Hike. One of the more fascinating trips is the evening Heritage of the Hoodoos Bus Tour which takes you into Dinosaur Park's badlands to explore the mysterious natural and cultural heritage of this landscape. Find out why it has had such a major impact on people throughout the world for centuries.

This is one of Canada's major attractions and, whilst man is here but a short time, the dinosaurs enjoyed millions of years of longevity. What a legacy they left us.

SEDLEC OSSUARY
**Zamecka 127, Kutna Hora,
Sedlec, Czech Republic**

The most bizarre and thought-provoking place you can ever visit is found at Sedlec in the Czech Republic. The Sedlec Ossuary (Czech: Kostnice Sedlec) is a Christian Chapel and contains approximately 40,000 human skeletons which have been turned into ornamentation to form furnishings and decorations for the chapel.

Henry, the Abbot of the Cistercian Monastery in Sedlec, was sent to visit the Holy Land in 1278 and returned with some 'holy' earth from Golgotha, which he then sprinkled over the cemetery. Word of this act spread like wildfire throughout Central Europe and Sedlec Cemetery became a most desirable place to be buried. Even people from abroad were buried here. Thousands of people died during the Bubonic Plague era (also known as the Black Death) and they were also buried here in the cemetery. With many thousands more people interred here following the Hussite Wars in the 15th century there was soon a need for the cemetery to be greatly enlarged.

A Gothic church was built in the centre of the cemetery which had an upper level and a lower chapel that was to be used as an ossuary for the mass graves that were unearthed during the construction of it. According to legend a half-blind monk was given the task of stacking all the bones of the exhumed skeletons in the chapel.

In 1870 a woodcarver named Rint was employed to put the vast piles of bones into order and the displays that he created are what you now see when you visit Sedlec Ossuary. On some of the skulls are deep markings that were the result of battle in the Hussite Wars. Creepy and somewhat disturbing, Rint's works also include a gigantic chandelier of bones hanging from the centre of the nave, garlands of skulls on the vaults, huge mounds of bones in each of the corners of the chapel and, quite chilling, his signature as creator of the works in a bone arrangement on a wall by the entrance. Numerous other works in bone, some artistic and some quite grotesque, can be seen here as the bone church is said to have been created to illustrate to visitors the shortness of life. However Rint, in his use of the remains of the 40,000 or so poor souls who are on display here, may be depriving them of a lasting peace that only the grave is said to offer.

*Tens of thousands of
human bones artistically
arranged for ornamentation.
A gruesome and thought
provoking sight.*

VIKING SPLASH TOURS

64-65 Patrick Street, Dublin, Ireland

Take a unique tour of famous Dublin by land and water in a vintage World War 2 amphibious vehicle called a 'DUKW", or 'Duck' as it is more commonly known. These vehicles weigh 7 tonnes and are 31ft long and 8ft wide. They were built by General Motors in the United States during World War 2. Your Viking Tour Captain - amusingly dressed as a tough Viking - tells you how the City came to be, and how the Vikings first settled here 1,000 years ago. So hang onto your hats as you plunge into the waters of the Grand Canal Basin on the water leg of your tour.

THE DUBLIN GHOST BUS TOUR

59 Upper O'Connell Street, Dublin, Ireland

Haunted houses, body-snatching, and Dracula's Dublin origins are all part of the Dublin Ghost Bus Tour. The fiends and devils of over 1,000 years of Dublin's turbulent history are brought to life on this macabre journey where a city of gaslight ghosts and horrendous legends will chill you to the bone. The Haunted Steps, and the traditions of the Irish wake are a few of the highlights of this superb tour that lasts over 2 hours.

Spooks, ghouls, and things that go bump in the night are all part of the attraction of the Dublin Ghost Bus Tour which will entertain you with tales, legends and sights of Dublin's infamous past.

TOBU WORLD SQUARE
209-1, Ohara, Fujihara-machi, Shioya-gun, Tochigi-ken, Japan

It took 5 years to complete Tobu World Square in Japan and the end result of this breathtaking attraction that opened in 1993 is a miniature marvel that has to be seen to be believed. Over 100 historic relics have been painstakingly constructed to precise 1/25th scale and look exact tiny replicas of the originals. The Roman Coliseum, Great Wall of China, Arc de Triomphe, Statue of Liberty, Big Ben, and Taj Mahal are just a few of the incredible reconstructions. In fact all of the world wonders are represented here in meticulous detail.

There are 140,000 tiny people at Tobu World Square - each individual and with unique features and functions. The attention to detail is truly astounding here with 100's of mini tourists gawking at most of the exhibits. Look carefully and you will even see tiny hot-dog sellers at Central Park, Marilyn Monroe at a window, and even wee bank robbers carrying their loot. Amazing!

WINDOW OF THE WORLD
Guangdong, Shenzhen, China

Not to be outdone by Japan, China's answer to Tobu World Square is a gigantic 480,000 sq.metre park that has sections covering Africa, America, Asia, Europe, and the Pacific. Landscapes, sculptures, cultural sites and much more are represented here including the pyramids of Egypt, the Grand Canyon of America, and the Sydney Opera House of Australia. Over 118 attractions illustrate the sights of the world from spectacular full scale to 1/100th scale. The Niagara Falls, and the 108 metre high Eiffel Tower are quite magnificent.

Human evolution is depicted on enormous 1,680 metre relief walls, 6 huge gates are representative of the birthplaces of other civilizations, and 'International Street' is a sight you will remember forever. There are numerous different forms of transport to get about this vast complex, whilst by night - when the lights come on - you will have an unforgettable experience.

The Roman Coliseum in meticulous miniature detail. Just one of the many attractions in the land of Tobu World Square.

book orders & suggestions

We hope you have enjoyed reading this book and will want to purchase other titles of Strangest Books. Please see the back cover for a brief description of other titles currently available in this series.

Our books can be purchased from all good book shops and a broad selection of other retailers. Alternatively, you may wish to visit our website where excerpts and images from other titles can be viewed free of charge, and books may be ordered direct.

We are always interested in hearing from readers with any comments or suggestions. If you would like to contact us please use the relevant e-mail link below.

e-mail direct

bookorders@strangestbooks.co.uk

suggestions@strangestbooks.co.uk

or visit our website at:

http://www.strangestbooks.co.uk